Houses

Rustic and Country Houses

Houses

AUTHOR
Francisco Asensio Cerver

PUBLISHING DIRECTOR
Paco Asensio

PROJECT COORDINATOR
Iván Bercedo (Arquitecto)

PROOFREADING
David Clough

DESIGN
Mireia Casanovas Soley

LAYOUT
Juan Prieto

PHOTOGRAPHERS
Richard Waite (*Casa Lundstrom*); Vincent Knapp (*Casa en Ibiza*); Lluís Casals (*Casa en el Maresme*); Thomas Linke (*Casa en Sundern*); Alain Weintraub (*Casa Seymour*); Lucinda Lambton (*Mansión Howe Green*); Erik Hesmerg (*Casa Van Veelen*); Deidi von Schaewen (*Casa en Idaho*); Lluís Casals (*Casa Hidalgo*); Simo Rista (*Casa en Hämeelinna*); Waltraud Krasen (*Casa en Taunus*); Jorge Hirata (*Casa Hélio Olga*)

ISBN: 2-88046-293-2

Published and distributed by ROTOVISION SA
Sheridan House
112-116A Western Road
Hove, East Sussex BN3 1DD
England
Tel. 1273 72 72 68
Fax 1273 72 72 69

Production and color separation in Singapore by
Provision Pte. Ltd.
Tel. (65) 334-7720
Fax. (65) 334-7721

Rustic and Country Houses

The idea of the country house immediately conjures up a whole series of images associated with proximity to nature and the desire to live in a landscape, to live life at a less hectic pace.

In today's society, centred on cities that impose their geometric landscape and their speed, the country implies a shift towards a different class of activity. Anyone who decides to build a house on a prairie or on the edge of a forest assumes an initial decision: the desire for a degree of isolation, the achievement of greater tranquility, and the beginning of a twofold journey: toward a heightened awareness of simple, irreducible things – mornings in the shade of the trees, afternoons by the river, the starry night sky, the sight of the horizon and the sun setting – and at the same time a gradual release from the webs of relationships and obligations which make up the urban fabric, and a move towards different facets of oneself, other personalities, which emerge as one´s rhythm of life slows down.

Nevertheless, above and beyond this common image we have, the country is also an actual place. Its houses have a precise, recognizable form. Houses in Germany's Black Forest, the hills of Iviza, the English countryside or the forests of Switzerland, houses that must withstand the cold of a Scandinavian winter or the tropical heat of Brazil, houses built on the desolate plains of Idaho or on the edge of the great conurbations of Japan, all have their own way of relating to nature, adapting to the landscape and expressing the motivations of those who live in them. This volume offers a panoramic view of country houses from far-flung places with a huge range of climates. They were all built in recent years, and while some hark back to the techniques and aesthetics of traditional architecture, others propose new and radical solutions. Each example provides us a with a uniquely different answer.

Yet perhaps a dialogue could be struck up between them... and to share the result would be extraordinarily enriching.

Rustic and Country Houses

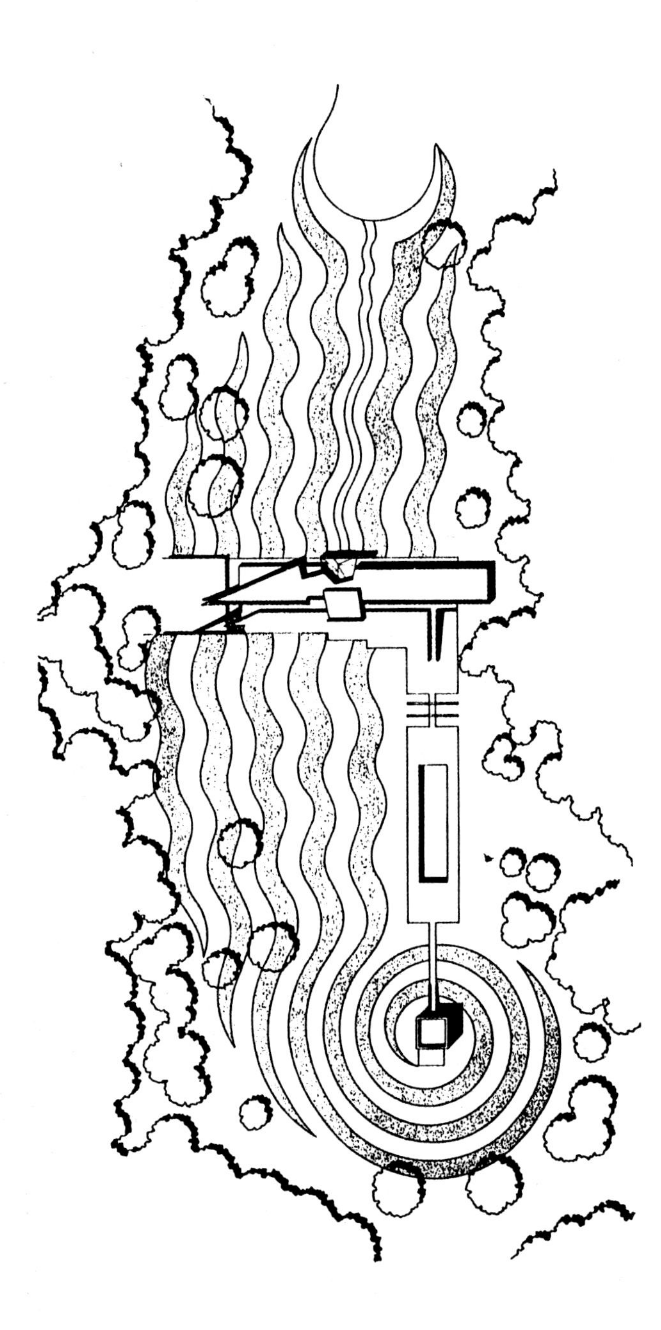

Situation plan.

Ludstrom House

David Connor

Villa Zapu is situated in one of the most important wine-producing regions of the United States, the Napa Valley. The Swiss owners, Thomas and Anna Lundstrom, at the same time that they began negotiations to construct their new residence, also decided to establish themselves as wine producers. Villa Zapu is a work charged with emotion, of surprising spaces and lyrical images which can only be understood from the effort and enthusiasm shared by the owners and the creators.

" There is something of anarchy and something of order. There are several cultural layers in Villa Zapu: architectonic, historical, practical, autobiographical and theatrical, which come together in all parts of the house ", states David.

Villa Zapu has an aspect somewhere between the monumental and the magical: the snaking path among the poppies and the wild wheat, combed by the wind, illuminated by night with punctual lamps in each one of the curves along the route, the huge entrance door that reminds one of a primitive temple, but which is somewhat out of place here, the undulating meadow, with strips of different greens like a confused, vegetable sea that forms whirlpools around the house, solitary, like a lighthouse in the middle of a wood or like a watchtower without a fortress, each image seems to have been stolen from the landscapes of a dream.

A view of the main entrance of the house. A hundred metres before reaching the house there is a side-road for vehicle access. One can only reach the main entrance by a narrow, twisting footpath.

The house is set on a small hill elevated above the spreading vineyards, in an open clearing between the trees which protect and isolate it from the valley. One arrives by a private road which ends at a roundabout in front of the main façade. An previous side-road allows one to drive up to one of the sides of the house where the garage can be found.

The main volume of the residence is a two-storey building having a very extensive plan, with a half-buried garage on one side.

The linear character of the building defines two clearly-distinct exterior areas. The front garden produces a representation of the entrance. The landscape gardeners and the architect have designed the space in a theatrical manner. As affirmed by the creators, the final spirit of this theatricalisation comes close to the architecture of Andrea Palladio. The visitor is converted into the protagonist of an episode that seems to have been taken from a epic drama: the arrival of the hero.

A general view of the rear façade and the garden, with the swimming pool in the foreground. According to the architect, they have attempted to make a renewed reading of the Venetian villas by Andrea Palladio in Villa Zapu.

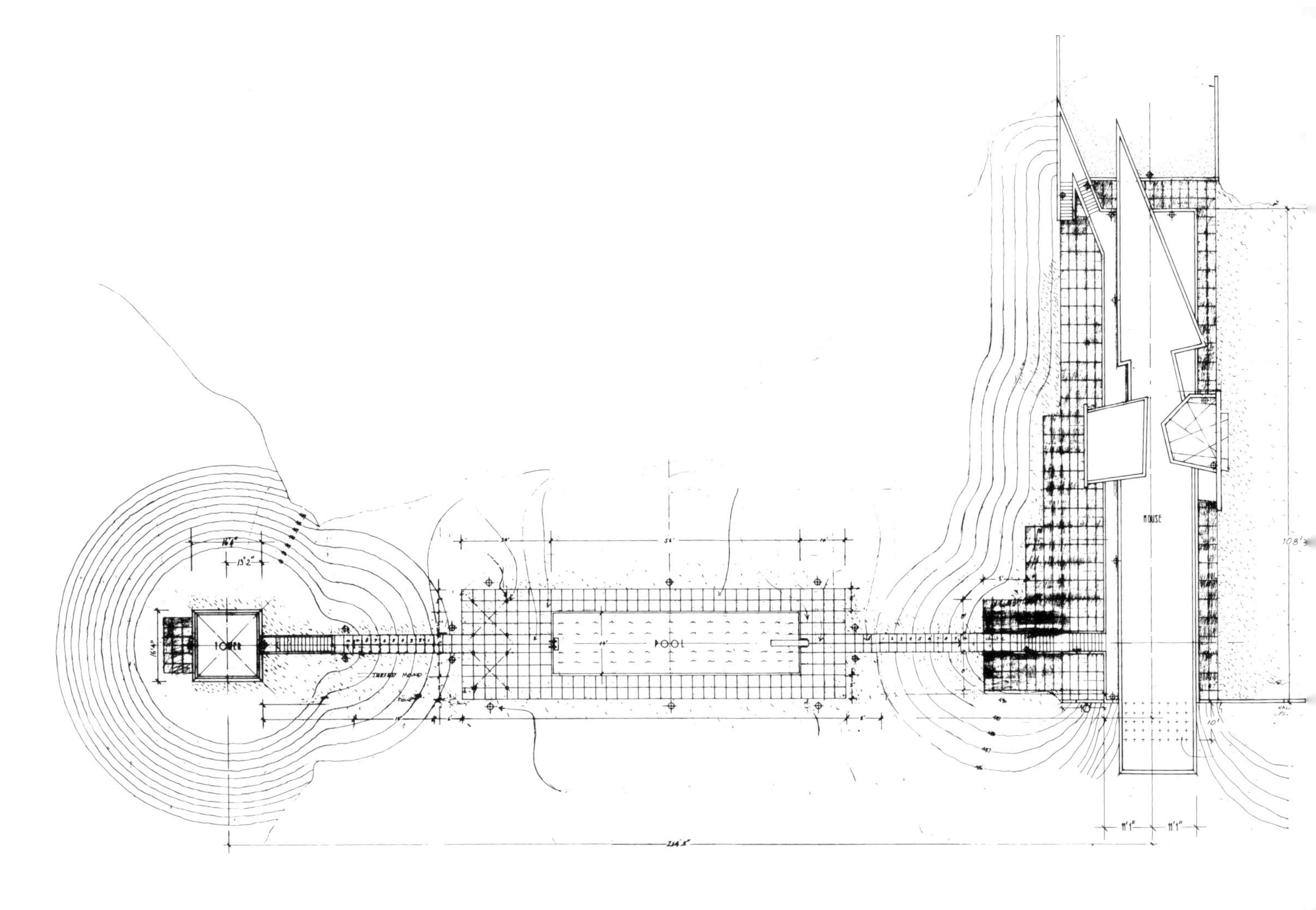
TOWER
POOL
HOUSE

An aerial view of the house. The garden was designed by Hargreaves Associates. The singular way of planting in parallel strips of high and low vegetation of different species is outstanding.

The guest tower, at the end of the swimming pool has great importance in the garden's order. It is a constant reference both from the garden and the house. Its hermetic surrealist aspect reminds one of the oneiric architecture of the paintings by Giorgio de Chirico.

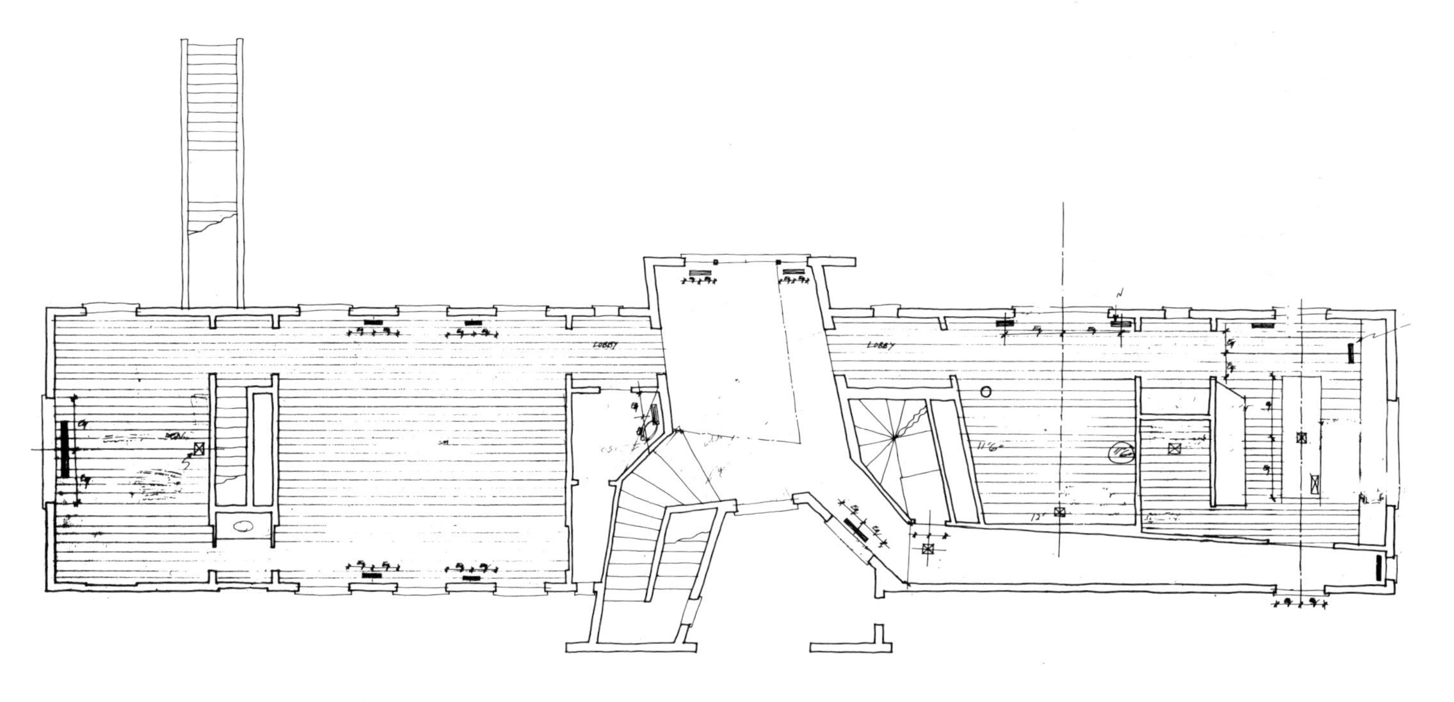

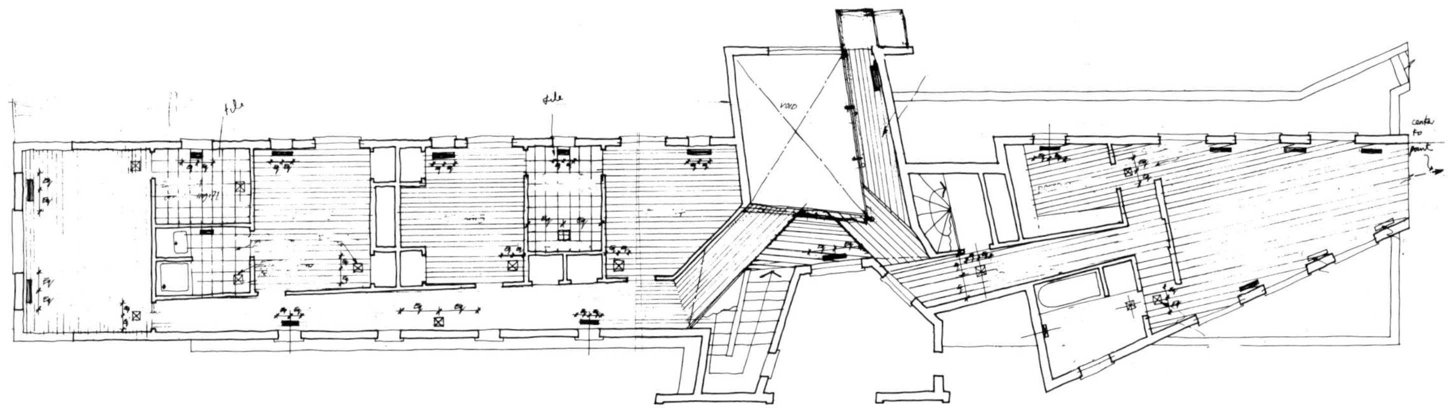

Ground and first floors.

Detail of the side façades. Both the volume of the master bedroom and the exterior stairway which descends from the first floor to the garden, overhang the building in the form of pointed wedges.

Night views of the garden and the main façade. The lighting is achieved thanks to punctual lamps placed in the perimeter of the paving and to floodlights which illuminate the façade.

However, unlike the Venetian villas of Palladio, where the façades recuperate the architecture of the classical temples, in Villa Zapu, the references are displaced towards oneiric landscapes. The rear garden has an intimate character. From one of the extremes of the house extends a perpendicular axis, displaced with respect to the centre of the house, on which is inscribed a long, narrow swimming pool, and a square-based tower, crowned with two horizontal flagpoles, from which two banners hang to the ground. It is inspired by the Tower of "San Gimigmano" in the Italian region of Tuscany. However, it reminds one mainly of the metaphysical and hermetic images painted by Giorgio di chirico: surrealistic architecture born from memory or myth.

Around the house, George Hargreaves has drawn a spiral of strips of vegetation that continue towards the house and descend on the undulating side of the hill in twisting curves.

On this and the following page, two aspects of the entrance and stairway to the first floor. The marble paving of the ground floor is cut into irregular shaped pieces. The parquet on the first floor has been laid in an oblique manner facing different directions.

The architect has introduced some aspects of abrupt geometry, which confer a great dynamism and vitality on the spaces.

Above, detail of the wedge-shaped bedroom. Some of the resources used in Villa Zapu possess an important theatrical component. The angles and sharp edges have succeeded in dramatising the spaces.

The strips are planted with native species having great resistance to drought and characterised by a notable degree of variation with the seasons.

In the interior organisation of the dwelling, the central element is of special importance. It brings together the entrance door, the access stairway to the first floor and a double space. This element not only divides the plan in half, but also introduces an abrupt geometry, of inclined walls and acute angles, which slightly disturb the straight forms of the rest of the building.

On the ground floor are found all the communal rooms of the dwelling: on one side the kitchen and the dining room, on the other, the living room. On the first floor are all the bedrooms. The central stairway and double space separate the master bedroom, with its corresponding bathroom and dressing room, from the rest of the bedrooms.

The master bedroom has a very accentuated triangular shape. The interior of this room, and

The design of the banisters helps to add dynamism to the central space. An oblique line divides the banister in two parts: one made of brick and plaster, painted white, the other of metal tubes and uprights. The stairway, the great door to the main entrance and a contiguous double space configure the centre of the house. The distribution of all the rooms in the dwelling is divided by the central element.

also the stairway or the corridors which communicate with the bedrooms have an expressionist character, which the space tends to dramatise. The passages, which are not parallel, but convergent, and the sections of the stairway of different width, which turn on themselves, confer a great vitality on the passing places and the intermediate spaces, and even give a certain degree of aggressiveness.

However, the windows follow a traditional style. Narrow and high, with two panes, of aluminium carpentry lacquered in white and of great simplicity. They are set out in series of three, combined in some cases with small square openings. Only on the sides are there some windows of a different type. As in the rest of the building, David Connor has tried to combine something of anarchy and something of order in the design of the details. ●

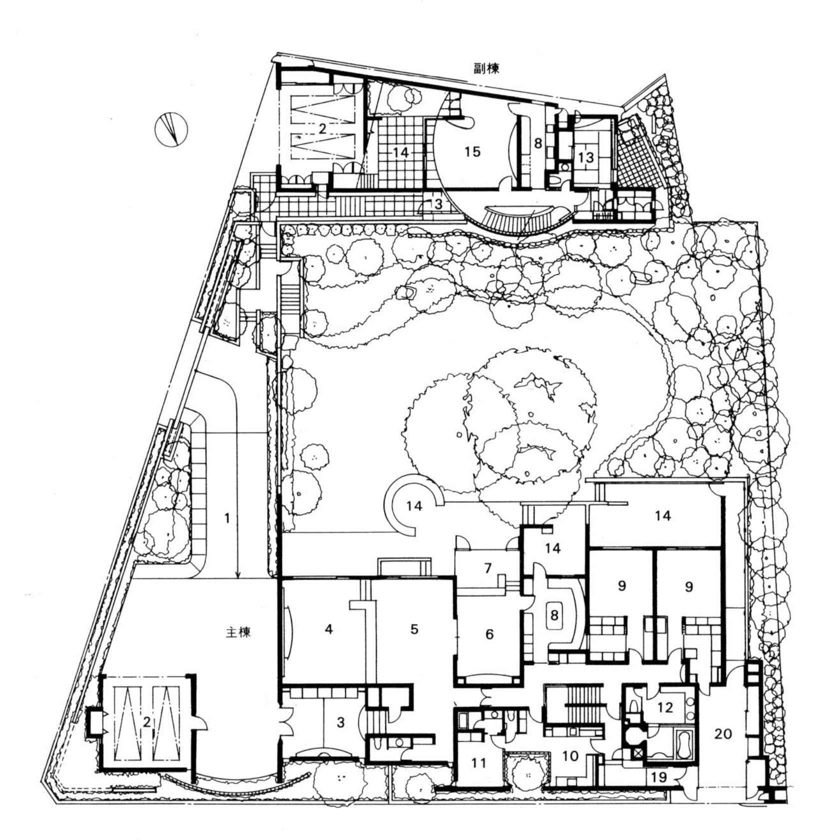

1階平面図　1:500

Takao Nodeki

This house is located not far from Tokyo, in a residential zone surrounded by trees and green belts. The relationship with nature is produced in a way that is completely different to that which occurs in the majority of western dwellings in this type of environment. Here, it is not nature which surrounds the residence, rather, it is the residence which surrounds nature. The lawns and trees occupy a central position, while the architecture constructs the borders and isolates the remains of an ancient wood.

The house is divided into two separate buildings, or, said in another way, comprises two single-family dwellings which correspond to two generations of the same family, who, even though they wish to live together, would also like to maintain a certain degree of independence. Thus, each of them contains its own living room, dining room, kitchen, bedrooms and garage.

The project was structured upon this duality. Each of the houses is placed at one and the other ends of the central garden: the main residence, with a total surface area of 800 m^2 to the north, and the daughter's, of 250 m^2 to the south, both having two floors. There is a wall on the east side, constructed along the slope of the vehicle access ramp, which joins both buildings, forming an architectonic perimeter that permits the limiting and controlling of the central garden.

One of the greatest worries of Takao Nodeki was to achieve spaces which were sufficiently isolated one from the other, in order to obtain maximum possible privacy and, at the same time, to have a direct relationship with the garden and that the illumination be natural. That is to say, to recover an intimate relationship with nature; with the change of the seasons; the variations in light and in the aspect of the trees, the transformation of colours, the birth of flowers and the appearance of fruit. The architecture must endeavour to allow us to experience all these transformations and, at the same time, that we do this in silent, introvert spaces where emotion is possible. This is the heritage of traditional Japanese architecture, the heritage which Takao Nodeki wishes to recover.

A watchword should prevail during the whole project, "closed yet open". The main building is structured on the base of a series of parallel walls which separate the rooms. These walls continue into the garden, but of lower height, forming an "L" which encloses a small terrace. In this way, each room has its own particular exterior space, somewhat elevated with respect to the central garden, which is accessed by going down three steps.

On the north façade, the one opposite the garden, are located all the services. The enclosure is not straight, but presents a series of offsets, walls where some slightly retreat or advance with respect to others, forming small flower beds with vegetation, through which light penetrates to the interior.

The daughter's house, of less surface area, possesses a somewhat different conception. The whole dwelling is organised around a central, double-height space occupied by the living room. This building is somewhat sunken with respect to the main house. The patios are smaller and more private.

Unlike the tendency in western country houses to include wide views of the landscape, in this house we find a different conception of nature, closer and more intimate. ●

A view of the vehicle access to the house. The residence is completely isolated from the exterior. There is a slight slope from the northern limit towards the south.

The access ramp to the garage. The wall on the left separates the interior, private garden access. The wall's offset has been used by the architect to install the illumination.

A view of the north façade. The circular wall of translucent glass blocks unites the garage with the entrance to the main house.

Details of the entrance to the daughter's residence. Although both houses form part of the same project, the families wished to maintain a certain independence.

A view of the garden façade of the main residence. The architects wished to maintain the existing trees. The wall has been finished in ceramic tiles.

Takao Nodeki

A general view of the hall of the main residence. The fine materials, marble, wood, the care with the illumination and the reduction to a minimum of the decorative elements, confer an elegant and tranquil atmosphere of to this room.

A view of the main bathroom of the house. A skylight allows this space to have natural light even though it is completely interior.

A general view of the hall of the main residence. The fine materials, marble, wood, the care with the illumination and the reduction to a minimum of the decorative elements, confer an elegant and tranquil atmosphere of to this room.

A view of the dining room. Warm, natural tones, ochres and light browns, have been used in almost all the rooms.

A general view of the living room. All the rooms of the ground floor have a close relationship with the garden.

Detail of the kitchen, with the central granite table. Here, in this case, colder finishes and polished surfaces have been used.

Detail of the stairway in the daughter's dwelling. Both natural and artificial light are given a detailed study. The treatment of the light and the transparencies are one of the project's constants.

A view of the entrance to the daughter's dwelling and of the starting point of the stairway, the circular form of the stairway and the trapezoidal profile of the plot introduce a different geometry into this house.

The living room of the daughter's house. Because of its situation, at the southern limit of the plot, this house is not orientated towards the central garden, rather to some small independent patios.

The house is organised around this central double space. The master bedroom has windows with views of the living room.

Detail of the main bedroom in the daughter's house, with the sliding partitions in the background.

The Tatami room is on the ground floor. It is a traditional space in a Japanese dwelling and is intended for multiple uses.

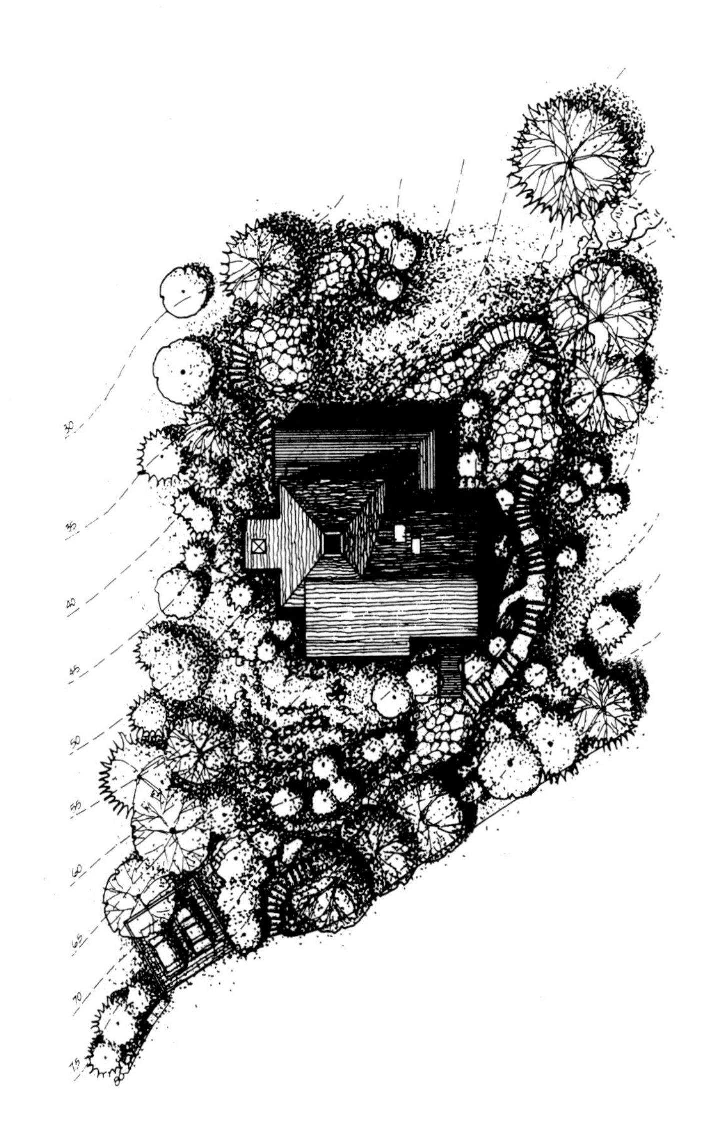
30
35
40
45
50
55
60
65
70
75

San Francisco Bay

Danadjieva / Koenig Associates

The Californian house over the San Francisco Bay appears within the natural texture of such a steep hillside that many thought could not be constructed on. Since it is sited somewhat away from the road, which serves as access from a higher level, its presence is not noticed among the trees, even though three floors rise above the ground. There is a small platform next to the road with room for two cars. From here, a twisting path of steps continues, descending obliquely through the dense vegetation, until it arrives at the first terrace built into the side which acts as a support for the entrance bridge to the house.

The exterior run continues forming other terraces between the topographic lines. They form small landings, constructed in the same way as the retaining walls, with native, serpentine rock, and seem to be an extension of the rocky formations of the hill.

The poor conditions of the ground for subsidence required deep foundations of piles that reached the solid bedrock. With the idea of reducing the cost of these expensive piles (the final total was 20), the main structure of the house attempts to minimise its area of contact on the ground, also reducing its impact on the existing topography. The needs of the programme caused an increase in the area of the upper two floors, adopting the solution of secondary, overhanging wooden structures. Such is the case of the grand terrace, the chimney recess, the dining room and the kitchen, all on the upper floor;

or the rooms on the middle floor. Since it is in a wooded area, the structure is therefore conceived as being a nucleus which functions as a trunk.

The distribution of the dwelling on three floors also corresponds to the differentiation of their activities. Thus, the upper or entrance floor is the public space for holding social activities; the middle level has a private character and work characterises the ground level.

The focal point of the project is the living room. If we could define the structural nucleus of the house as being divided into two halves by the stairway, then the living room would completely occupy the northern half. This space would also be the crowning glory; carpets, cushions, fittings and furniture are placed on the parquet; its walls are covered with pine-wood panels and describe the exterior countryside; and the tree-like structure which covers its perimeter seems to be

From among the rocks spring ferns, elements of the countryside. Intervention looks after all the details of the location. The weeds were removed to strengthen the growth of the native wild flowers of the Bay. Among them, the fragile and almost extinct Clarkia rose returns to life.

The materials, the structure, the warm glow and the shadows of the house integrate perfectly into the colourful surroundings of the wood.

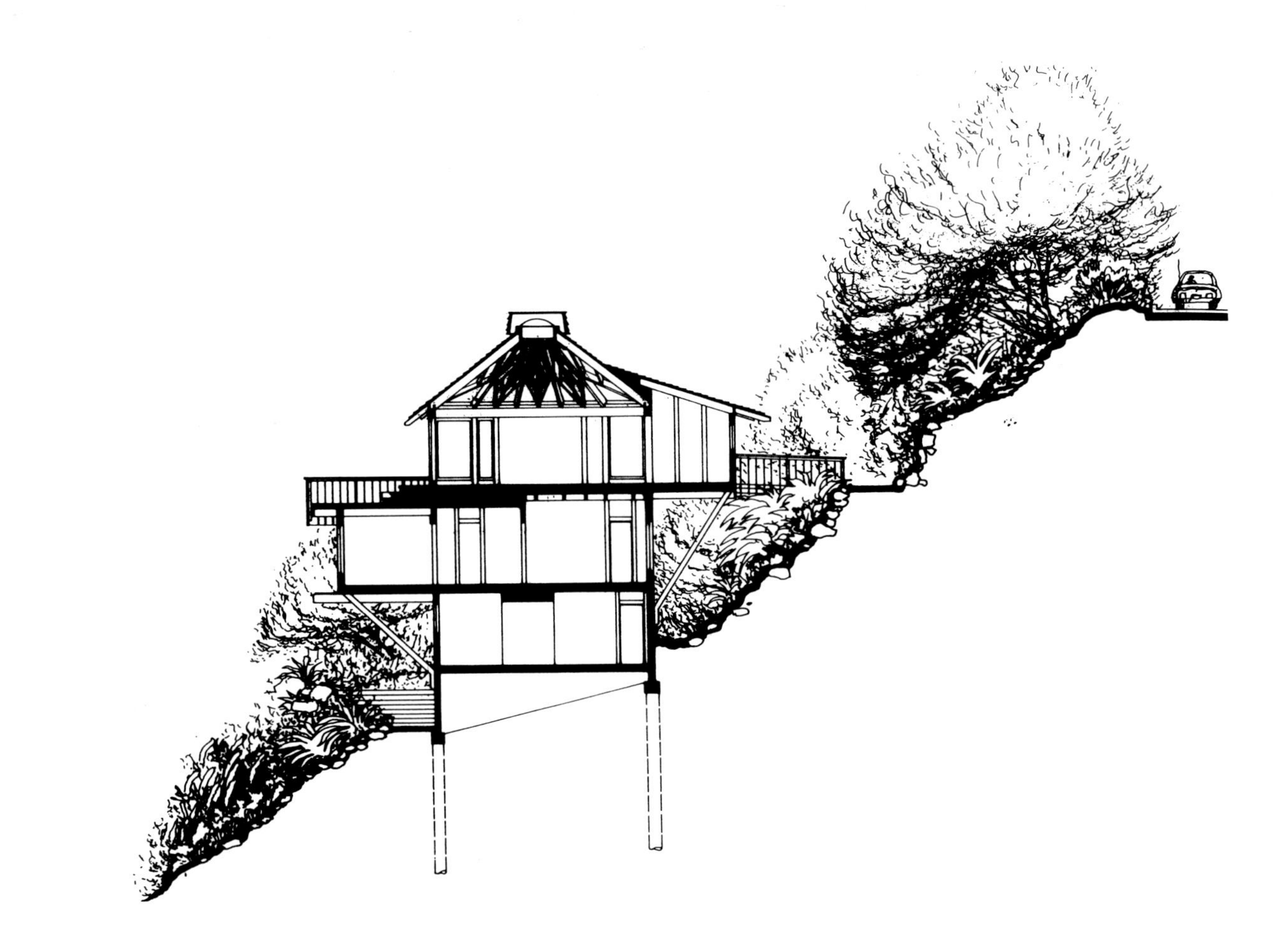

Section. From the main structure, embedded in the ground, the projecting framework emerges, so that the house appears to rise above its surroundings, maintaining the existing topography practically intact.

The living room, a carpeted space with original objects, with views out over the Bay, and in which reigns the warmth of wood; the grand space under the rich and illuminated structure of the roof.

In remembrance of the San Francisco Bay, the air vent from an old boat was re-used in the chimney recess. The cushions lie on the floor, scattered around the fire.

In a corner of the living room, rustic wood shelving is used to display dazzling collections of objects (Greek Orthodox icons, silver cups or antique Victorian doorknobs), and the memory of the owner's European heritage.

Large earthen jars on the terrace; living nature between lines; the handrail and the horizon.

Next to the entrance, one of the house's multiple large windows which frames views of the hillside and contributes, with its connection with nature, to the exploitation of energy

The upper or entrance floor, it acts as a public space for family meetings and pastimes. It includes the living room, the chimney recess, the dining room, the kitchen and the piano room.

The middle floor contains the private rooms together with the breakfast room and the bedrooms.

The lower floor has been designed as a work area, with a study, a library and a kitchen. It also contains a space for use as a storeroom. Its perimeter helps in the understanding of the higher parts of the building by the superposition of the upper floors.

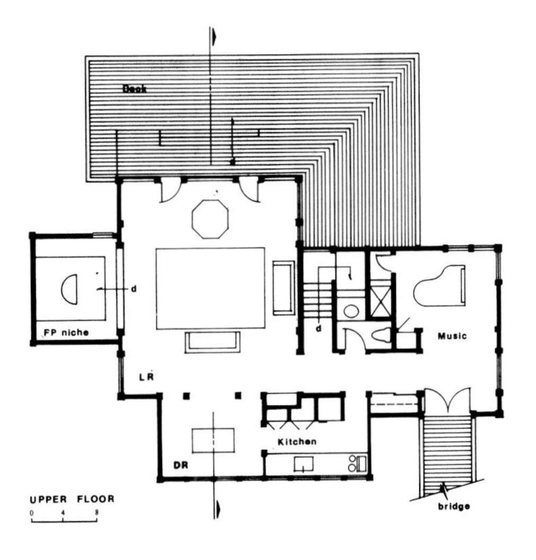
Deck
d
FP niche
d
Music
LR
Kitchen
DR
bridge
UPPER FLOOR
0 4 8

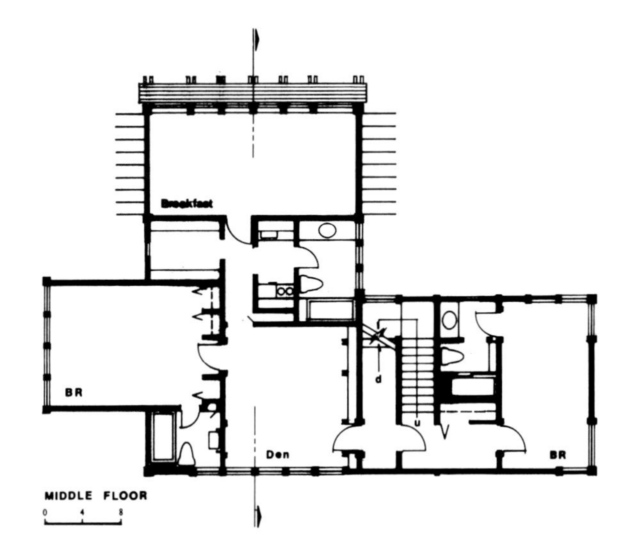
Breakfast
BR
d
u
Den
BR
MIDDLE FLOOR
0 4 8

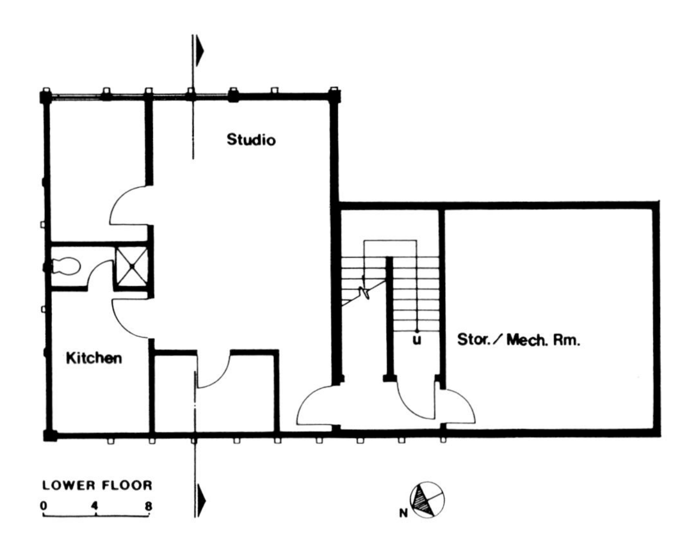
Studio
Kitchen
u
Stor. / Mech. Rm.
LOWER FLOOR
0 4 8
N

suspended from the highest point of the ceiling, making it still more magnificent. Even though it is just a simple hipped roof from the outside, when underneath it, one has the sensation of being protected by the very laws of nature in a kind of cabin.

The colour and texture of the wood are exalted by the soft glow of the hidden incandescent lamps, accentuating the expressive form of the ceiling and emphasising the natural warmth of the material. The inherent beauty of the materials from the wood form nearly all the surfaces of the house.

The design philosophy of Danadjieva & Koenig Associates is born from the belief that a residence should reflect the specific tradition of its locality and also the necessities and personalities of its owners. The project's interior insinuates the European heritage of its owner and the tradition of the San Francisco Bay. But, above all, this house reflects and understands the character of the location, in its most poetic sense. •

"Just as a tree gathers its burden on its trunk and dynamically responds to the forces of nature, so does the house by directing its load towards its perimeter. Both, the tree and the roof, recognise the rules to which they have to submit."
(Gary Hansen, AIA, RIBA)

Inspired by the architecture of Eastern Europe, the roof's structure is formed by a system of radial beams set into a rectilinear compression ring.

Works model and plan drawing of the roof structure. In concept, it forms the inverted crown of a tree.

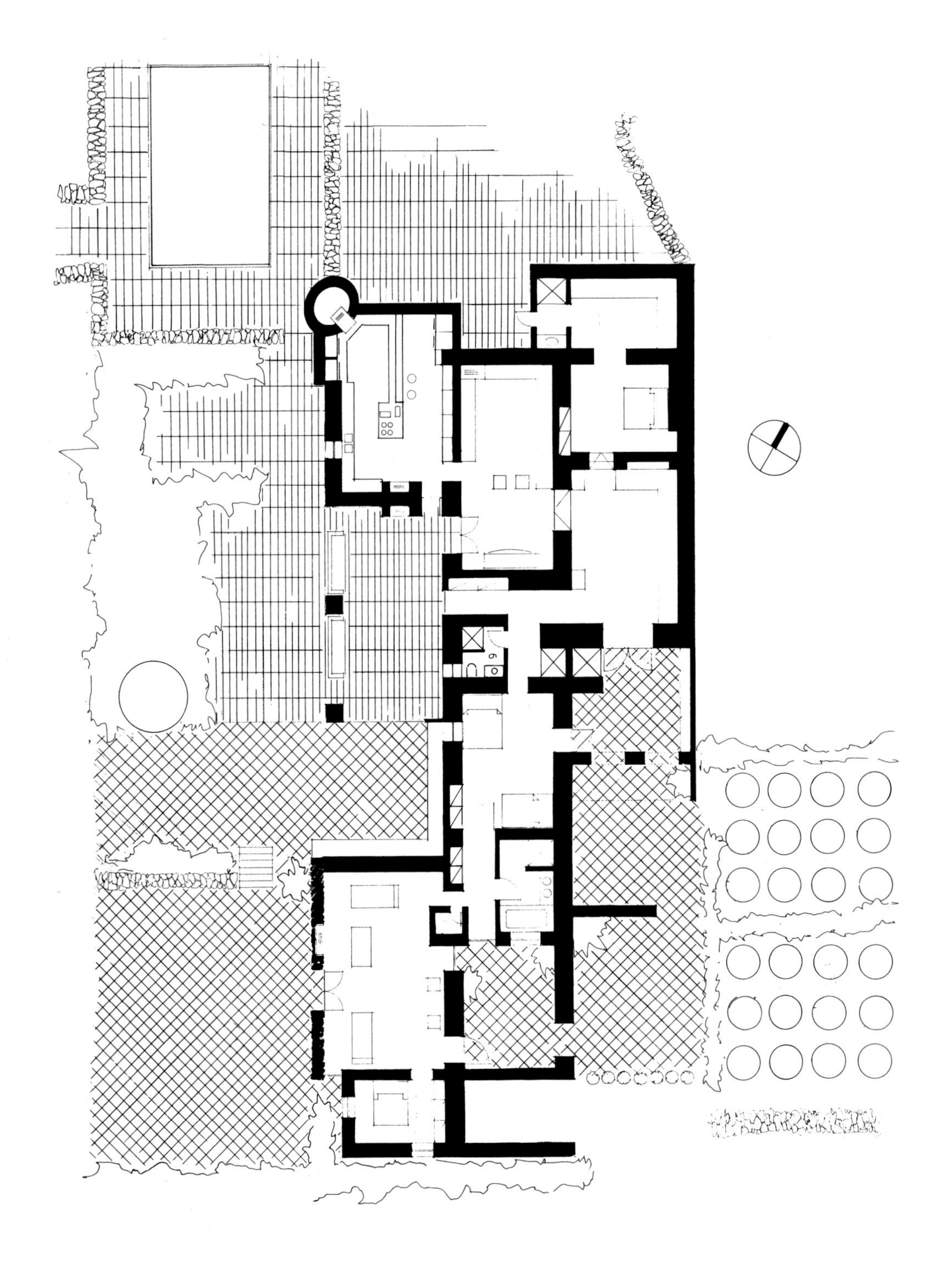

General plan of the ground floor.

House in Ibiza

Anna Golin

The grounds of this house are sited on a small hill, between giant prickly pears and oleanders that have grown for years between the white-washed walls of the constructions, creating a landscape which is inseparable from the Mediterranean image. In the mountains of Ibiza (Spain), which rise in front of the sea, on a plot with views of the island's port, there has been a small church here since the seventeenth century, which was restored and amplified by the Swiss architect Anna Golin, with the idea of using it as a dwelling.

The remodelling has tried to conserve the essential parts of the old building by carrying out a conscientious process of rehabilitation and adaptation. The necessary amplification has been done with the traditional building techniques of the area, and because of this, it is practically impossible to note the differences between the recent construction and the old church. Moreover, in the architecture of the region, the slow addition of new volumes, according to the necessities of the owners, is common, so that the majority of the houses grow alongside the families, drawing heterogeneous volumes and superimposed forms which integrate into the irregular topography of the island. Anna Golin's project recovers the irregular lines, the volumes which adapt themselves to the unevenness of the ground and which reproduce once again the

The project of Anna Golin, to respect the architectonic forms of the existing building, a small seventeenth century church.

The architect adds the geometric and the traditional, the austere and the profound, the hermetic and the nearby.

On the following page, a general view of the house. The white-washed walls with rounded edges and narrow openings adapt themselves to the abrupt topography of the Ibizan mountains.

A view of the patio in the guest area, with the volume of the master bedroom silhouetted against the sky in the background.

On the left, detail of the terrace contiguous to the swimming pool. The architect has used the traditional construction techniques of the Balearic Islands.

Aspect of the terrace of the west façade. It is one of the main spaces of the house. It functions as an authentic outside living room.

natural continuity of the landscape through the round-edged, white-washed walls that are superimposed one on the other. A building of complex forms that the even white-wash and the bold, superimposed shadows which blur the limits of each volume, manage to unify. The openings are small and narrow to protect the interior from the implacable Mediterranean summer sun. One perceives the dark lines and points on the white background as simple geometrical marks.

This capacity of Mediterranean architecture to produce forms of great geometrical simplicity had already been discovered by Le Corbusier and the first generation of modern architects. Anna Golin adds the geometrical and the traditional to unfold all the evocative potential of this architecture, conceived almost as an inhabitable sculpture.

The white block of the bedroom stands out like a monolith rising towards the sky, with a narrow window with fixed panes. On the right, is

the entrance through a two-storey body of large arches. The porch is big, with a traditional form made from juniper wood beams. From here one can see the port of Ibiza. In front of the entrance are a few clay pots and jars, an ancient white-washed water tank, bundles of dry olive branches, wickerwork baskets, they occupy the space as if it were a stage setting, playing the role of an identity which wishes to present itself.

On the west façade, Anna Golin has incorporated a terrace with a cane pergola that filters the sun's rays. Two long, white brick benches close off the space. A series of successive terraces at different levels go around the house. The swimming pool is in the largest of them, surrounded by palm trees and a stone wall with bougainvillaea. The benches which are backed onto the walls offer seats shaded by the vegetation.

The interior distribution is completely remote from the schematism and optimisation of the

An aspect of the room contiguous to the master bedroom. The light penetrates through the arches of the façade.

Detail of the living room. At the back one can see the table of the main terrace of the house, orientated to the west.

Detail of one of the areas in the guests' living room. The table is made of two beams from a boat on a simple steel structure.

The interior finishes are of great simplicity. The lack of furniture acquires the same value as the paintings and sculptured pieces in their surroundings.

majority of current constructions. The thick loadbearing walls define reduced and closed spaces, of high ceilings with visible, irregular wooden beams. The rooms are related with a different logic, that of union. The spaces succeed each other like episodes, and, although the real isolation between the rooms is large, the sensation of remoteness of the rooms from one extreme of the house with respect to the other is even greater.

The unpolished, ceramic tile paving and the walls, white-washed from floor to ceiling, with hardly any furniture, without doors in the majority of the rooms, even adding steps in the way of benches or tables: it all transmits an atmosphere of simplicity and veracity. Rooms in shadow, with narrow openings, fresh in the summer.

The hall, the living room and the kitchen are of similar size. The distribution is determined by the hierarchy of the spaces. The living room is linked both with the hall and the kitchen and with the covered terrace of the west façade, which, in fact, functions as the authentic main space of the house.

All the bathrooms of the house are tiled in blue. In the guests' bathroom, a chrome washstand has been mounted on a glass surface in an inverse operation of that of Marcel Duchamp, with the intention of modifying the usual aspect of this type of bathroom fitting, almost converting it into a work of art.

The guests' bedrooms are organised in a communal area around a living room which has a 3-metre-long table made of two wooden beams from a boat, mounted on an iron trestle.

In a certain way, both the furniture and the continuous presence of pieces of sculpture, reveal to us the feeling of the reform carried out by the Swiss architect: the desire to displace the domestic space towards a purely artistic significance. ●

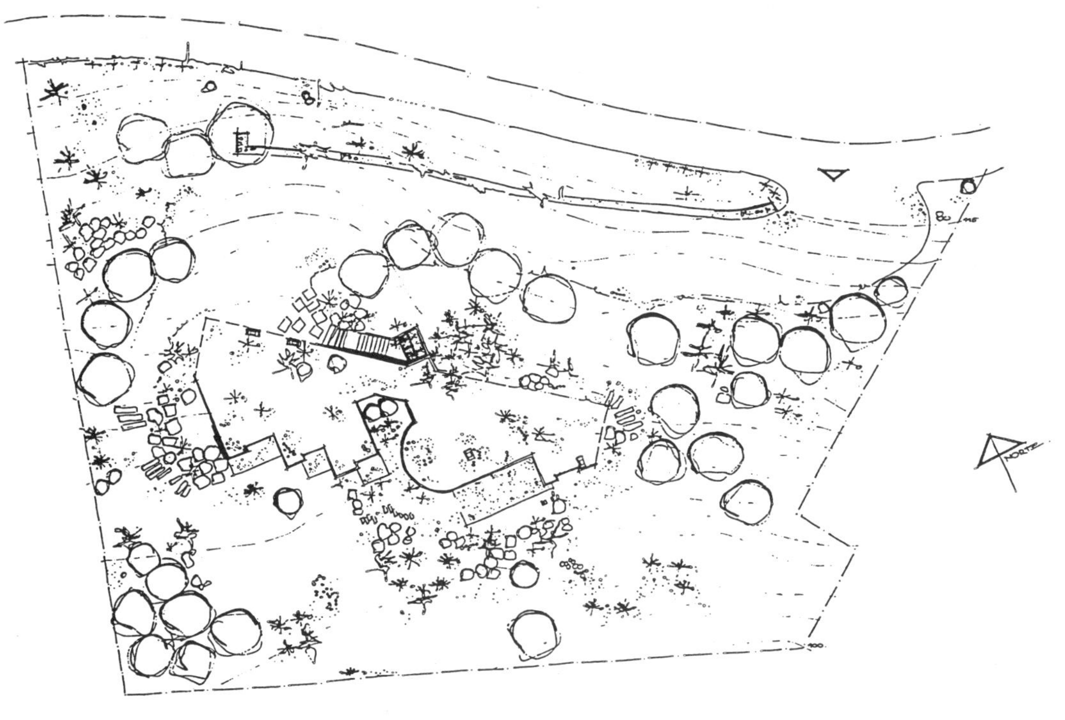

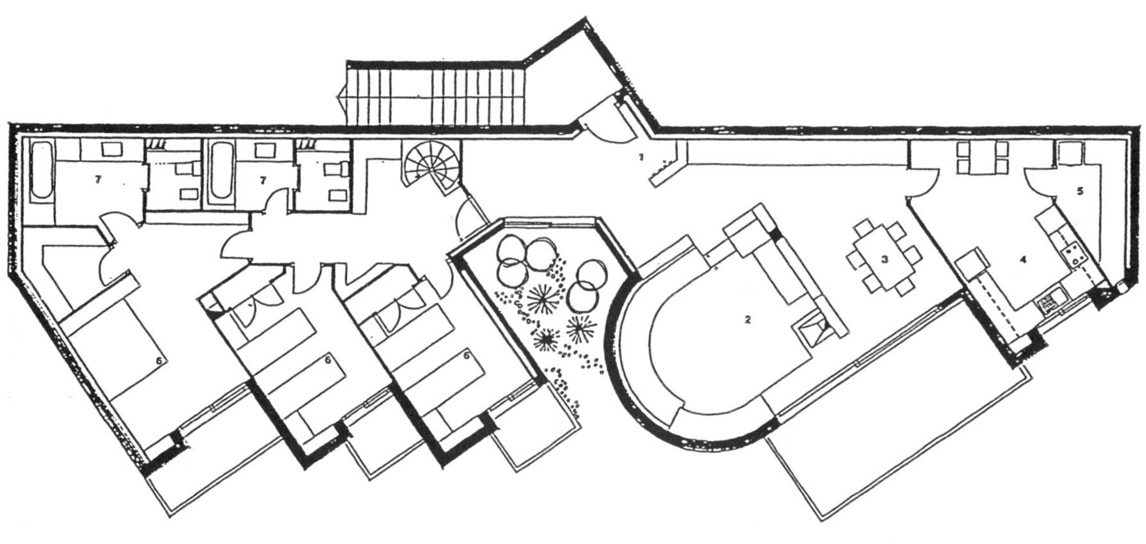
1
2
3
4
5
6
7
0 1 2 3 4 5

Maresme

Javier Barba

In the Catalan Maresme region, this house is *hidden* beside the highway which links the village of Sant Andreu de Llavaneres with Sant Vicenç de Montalt. The construction is so carefully integrated into the site that as time passes it will eventually be indistinguishable from its surroundings. The abundant vegetation of this Mediterranean environment, and the proximity of the sea were the basic factors which influenced the conception of the unusual building.

The architect had to adapt the design to the demanding topographical conditions of a 2,000 m^2 site. The steep slope and long shape formed what was virtually a ravine filled with trees and brushwood. It was the configuration of this site which suggested the idea of building a house *inside* the mountain, with a flat roof which would serve as a garden, so that the building would be perfectly integrated into the setting. The site was therefore levelled with earth taken from the excavation, and a rubble retaining wall was built from one side to the other. In this way, an open space for a front garden was also obtained.

This contextualisation of the dwelling in its environment culminated in the construction of a underground structure covered with earth and planted with Mediterranean vegetation. With this design solution, Barba has managed to protect the occupants from the noise of a busy road only 20

metres away, and also gained a great deal of free thermal insulation.

The long narrow ground plan of the house is completely irregular on one side, while on the other, it describes a prolonged straight line. The main entrance to the house is at the centre of this line. Seen from the outside, the entrance, which is partly camouflaged by vegetation, diminishes the importance of the residence behind it. On this side, the exterior facade is practically nonexistent, since the house is built into the mountain.

The southern facade, on the other hand is open to the exterior and exposed to the sunlight throughout the day. Visually it is divided into two sections: on the western side, the walls are interrupted to create a stepped structure and a terrace on each one of the insets created. On the opposite side, the curvilinear east wing is a half-circle, extended on one side to form the main part of the elevation formed by large glass surfaces in front of a porch. The porch can be covered with a canvas roof supported by a metal pole. Remaining true to his building philosophy Javier Barba finished the exterior with broken concrete because its colour is similar to that of the granite of the mountainside.

A section of the garden curves inwards between the two sections of the south facade, narrowing the centre of the floor plan. This device not only exemplifies the architect's precepts by clearly introducing nature into the house, but also achieves an exterior structural separation which favours the interior design of the house.

The flat roof is a garden so shat the building integrated into its setting.

On this facade the walls are interrupted to create a stepped structure and a terrace on each one of the insets created.

The southem facade is open to the exterior and exposed throughout the day to the sunlight.

View of the entrance.

The three bedrooms are laid out in the stepped tripartite structure in the west wing. They are rectangular and laid out side by side, so that each one has a small terrace. The main living room of the house is adjacent to these rooms, only separated from them by the small garden cavity. This room occupies the east wing, together with the dining room and kitchen.

In the living room, the architect has designed a long, narrow, rectangular window occupying the entire perimeter of the semicircular wall, providing a panoramic view of the garden and the mountain surrounding the house. This large room, which comprises both the living and dining areas, commands a view of the pool surrounded by pine trees and greenery. Viewed from above, the pool echoes the Mediterranean in front of the house. The living room receives additional light from the large glass door that opens on to the porch.

The floor on the house is terra-cotta *tiling* from Aragon, and all the walls are plastered and painted white except for those in the main living room, where the raw concrete was painted white. These materials transform the interior of the house into a large and comfortable space with clean lines where all of the furnishing is simple and appropriate.

Architecture should be seen as a continuation of nature and not as an intrusion. Javier Barba has once again designed an unusual house integrated into its natural context which with the passage of time will become indistinguishable from the landscape. •

The irregular shaped swimming pool is surrounded by pine trees and greenery.

The construction is so carefully integrated into the site that as time passes it will eventually become indistinguishable from its surroundings.

The living room is a semicircular shape and is open to the exterior.

A section of the garden curves inwards between the two sides of the south facade, narrowing the centre of the floor plan.

View of the porch in front of the living room sheltered by a canvas roof supported by a metal pole.

The flooring all over the house is Aragon tiling or terra-cotta, and the walls are plastered and painted white.

View of the living room. The furniture is perfectly adapted to tge semicircular walls of the room.

Hearth area. The walls of the living room are whitewashed concrete.

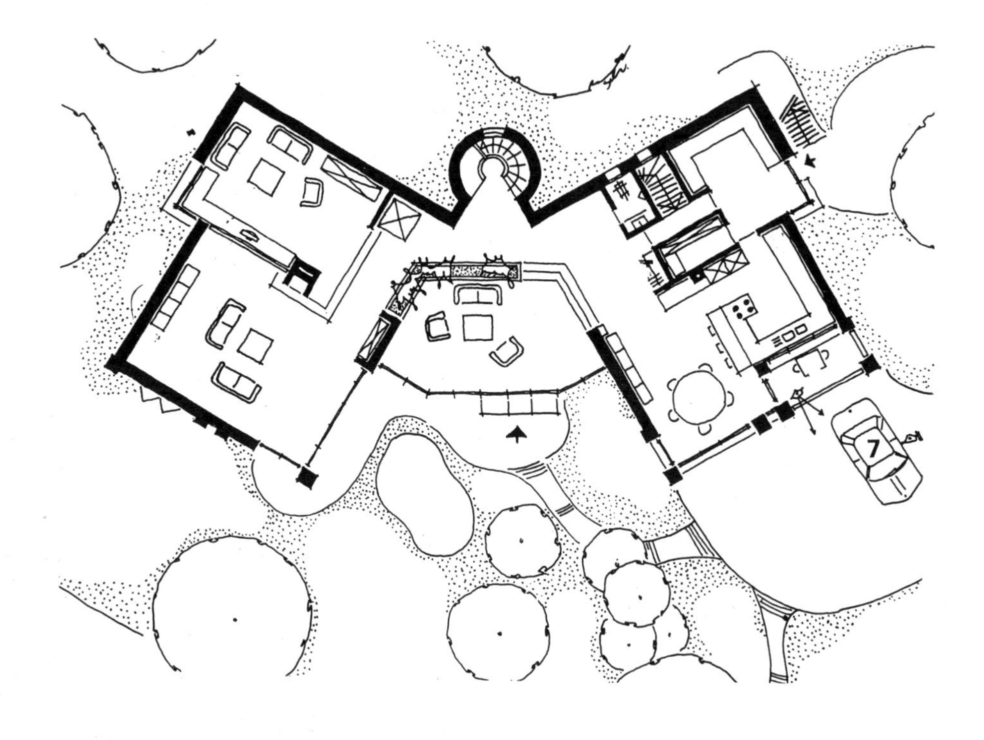

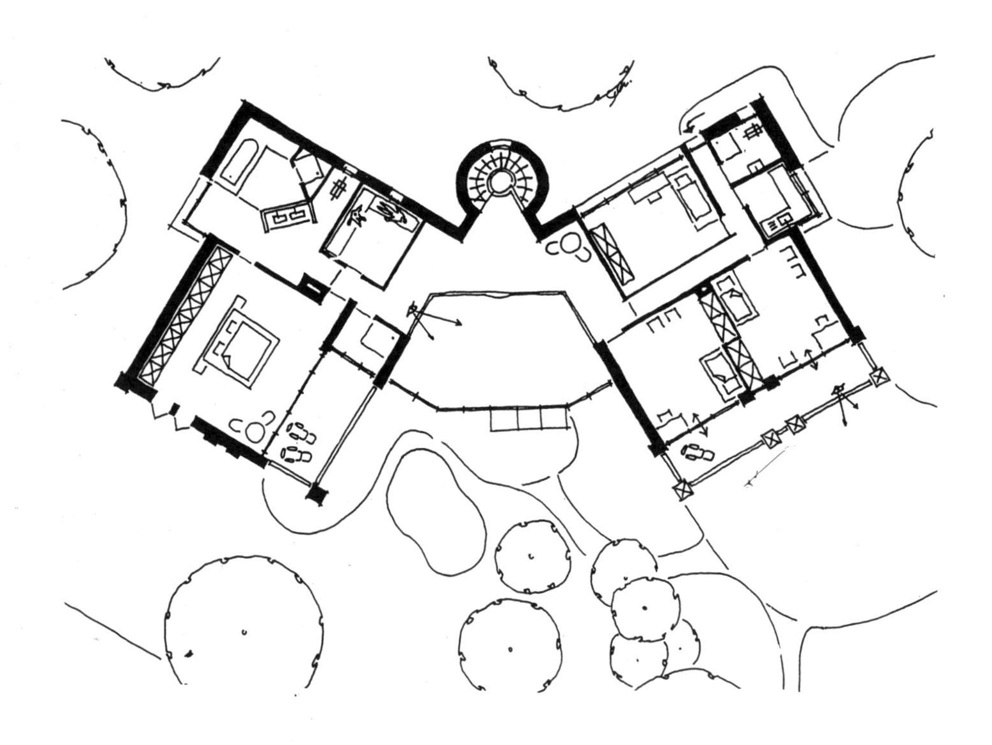

House in Sundern

Bernd Schwens

The grounds on which the house stands are situated in the small, Swiss locality of Sundern, in Hochsauerland, within a leafy, deciduous wood, close to a protected area of underground water. Although the plot has an area of 1,500 m^2, the steep slope which runs in a northeast-southeast direction made the siting of the house, in accordance with the wishes of the owners, very difficult. Precisely for this reason is Bernd Schwens' project surprising, he has been able to design a house which completely adapts to the topography and integrates itself into the heart of the wood, where it was only necessary to cut down three small trees.

The building consists of two symmetrical volumes, both of square plan, of different heights: one with two floors and the other with three. Both blocks are turned, one with respect to the other, in a fan-shape, so that the whole house opens out onto views of the valley on the other side of the wood. A spiral staircase joins them vertically as if it were a hinge. A small garden has been created in the angle which they form and covered with a glass structure, just like a greenhouse. This central space forms the very heart of the building and in a certain way expresses the overall spirit of the home. The plan view of the house looks like a bird which is spreading its wings.

Bernd Schwens has designed a series of terraces around the house, which interconnect the interior spaces of the different floors.

A view of the pedestrian access. An inside garden, covered by a glass structure as if it were a greenhouse, occupies the centre of the house. The inside garden is set in the angle formed by the two symmetrical cubic blocks which make up the building and was designed as a prolongation of the exuberant exterior vegetation.

Bernd Schwen has converted the interconnecting spaces of the project into the main area of the house, where its image is configured. This double-height space is not only where the handrails, the stairs or the entrances to the bedrooms come together, but also this same space opens out to give character to the living room, the dining room, the kitchen and even to the master bedroom. The way of opening out to the light, of including vegetation in the very definition of the spaces, and of placing the rooms on different levels, repeats itself throughout the house.

The architect has chosen white as the uniform colour both for the exterior and the interiors. Bernd Schwens does not consider the contrasts of different materials or colours as important as the possibilities that white offers when playing with light, the shadows thrown by the trees, the highlights and continuous movements of the shadows of the indoor plants on the floor and the walls.

In fact, this space which stands out between the two cubic volumes is no more than just a part of this exterior exuberance that the architect wanted to capture. When one looks at the ground floor, one cannot state with complete certainty if it is an extra room or a terrace. From outside it looks like a greenhouse which has been built *a posteriori* and one has the impression of having gone through a wood when going from the living room to the dining room.

Although the ground floor of the house presents a clear symmetry, the slope of the ground and the large number of trees, prevent an evident perception of this. However, the peculiarities of a symmetrical conception, the duality of space, the dialectic set up between both sides, and the existence of a central pivot, all live together.

The two blocks are of the same height. That is, the roof is built on a single plane. However, the southern block has an extra, half-buried floor,

Access is by a narrow path which goes around the house between the trees. The dwelling is adapted to the abrupt topography of the ground, so it is difficult to appreciate the symmetry of the plan from the outside.

The glass surfaces are constructed from "AW" aluminium frames and "Vegla-i-plus" double glazing to increase the thermal insulation.

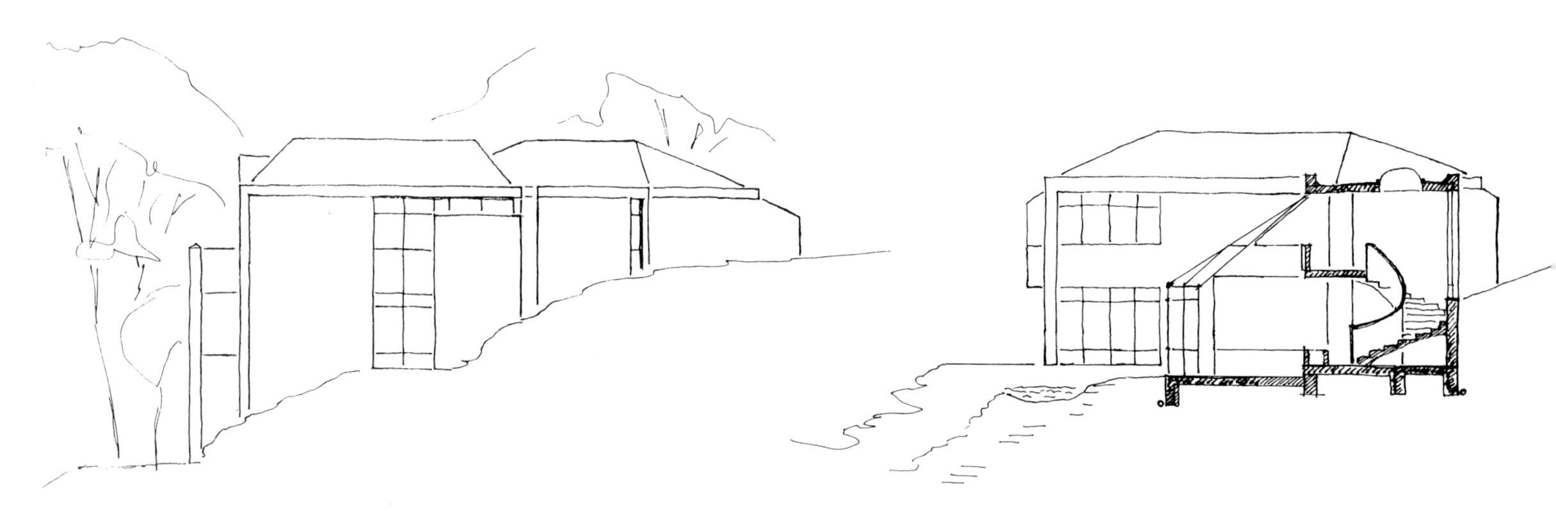

where the garage and services are sited, taking advantage of the slope of the ground.

From the small, paved esplanade in front of the garage, access on foot is by way of a small path which climbs up to the central, glazed garden, goes around the first block and continues climbing through the trees. From the inside garden, which also acts as a reception hall, one can reach both the dining room on one side, and the living room in the opposite block. The dining room is directly connected to the kitchen, only being separated by a counter. Between both spaces, Bernd Schwens has included a terrace for breakfasting. The living room is divided into two different levels, one open to the garden and the other, higher and secluded, intended as an area for watching television.

The spiral staircase leads to the highest part of the dwelling, where all the bedrooms are. A balcony over the double space of the inside garden separates, and at the same time joins, the

A view of the inside garden, which is not only the dwelling's entrance hall, but also the space which opens out onto all the rooms in the house, forming its authentic heart

On the following page, a view of the greenhouse from the balcony of the ground floor. As can be appreciated, the vegetation does not add to the architecture, but the two carry out a dialogue.

A partial view of the lounge, with the chimney in the foreground. The floor is covered with grey carpeting and the air-conditioning is produced through air conduits fitted into the floor.

Partial views of the staircase and the connecting spaces. The relationship between the different areas is in a flowing manner, through the inside, central garden.

children's area with the master bedroom area with its own bathroom and sauna.

A glass element overhangs the plane of the façade on the wings of both blocks. On the upper floor, this element must recuperate the line of the façade so that the bathrooms, both of the master bedroom and the children's area, open up to the sky via a glass structure which allows the clouds to be seen through the tree-tops from the baths.

The floor is covered with grey carpeting, except in the damp areas and the inside garden, which have been paved with the same ceramic tiles as the terrace so as to achieve a visual continuity. Both blocks have an independent hipped roof, while the central zone has a flat roof.

Bernd Schwens has established a series of terraces around the house which allow access to the outside from any floor. In this way, the desire to maintain permanent contact with wood is repeated in each particular area: the kitchen, the master bedroom the children's area, ... ●

Detail of the living room. The arrangement of the furniture has been carried out according to the different illumination levels of the spaces.

The kitchen and the dining room are only separated by a counter. On the ground floor, from the living room to the kitchen, from one extreme of the house to the other, there are no doors.

The kitchen and the dining room are only divided by a counter. On the ground floor, from the living room to the kitchen, from one end of the house to the other, there are no doors.

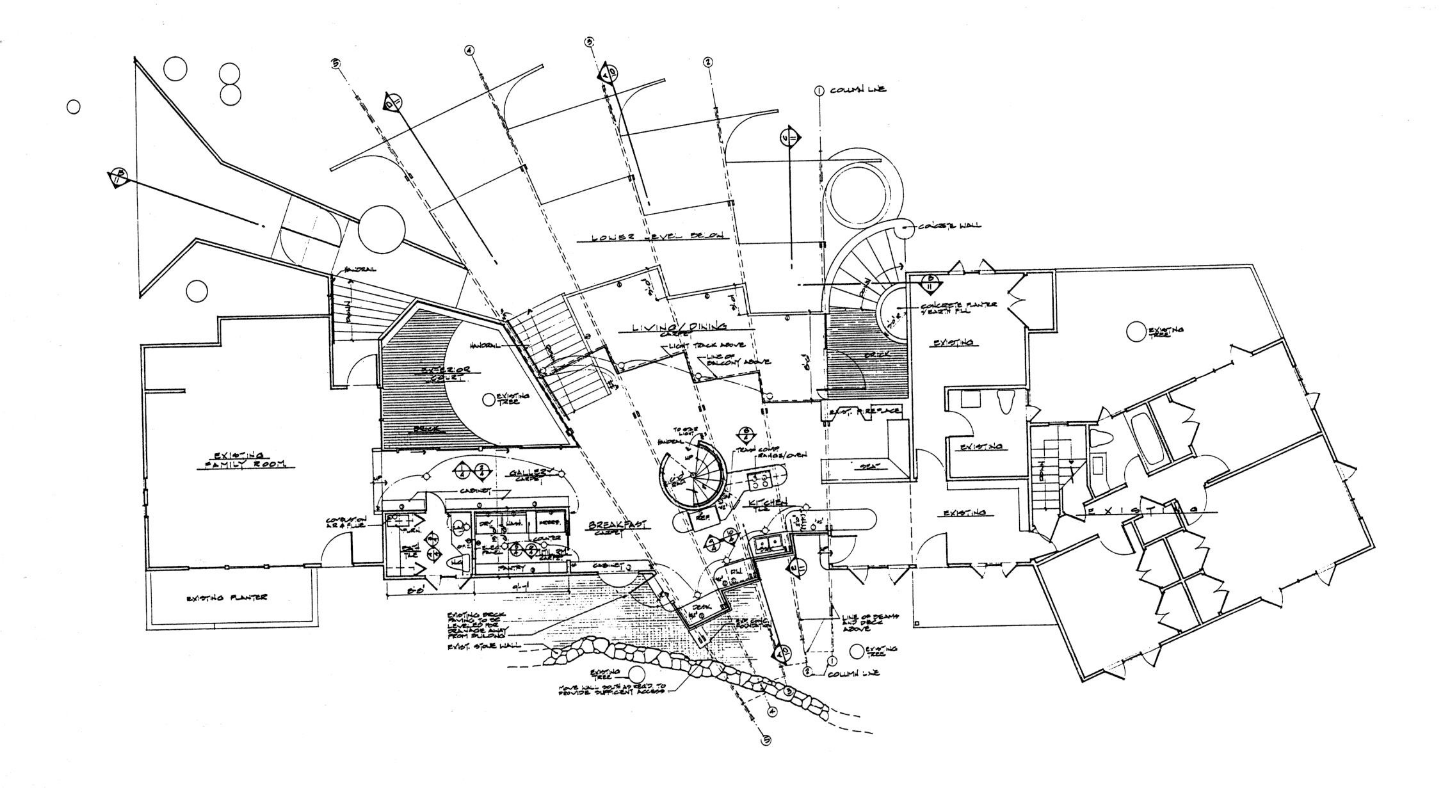

COLUMN LINE
CONCRETE WALL
LOWER LEVEL BELOW
LIVING/DINING
HANDRAIL
EXTERIOR COURT
EXISTING TREE
BRICK
EXISTING FAMILY ROOM
GALLERY
BREAKFAST
KITCHEN
CABINET
PANTRY
EXISTING PLANTER
EXISTING
SEAT
DECK
EXIST. STONE WALL

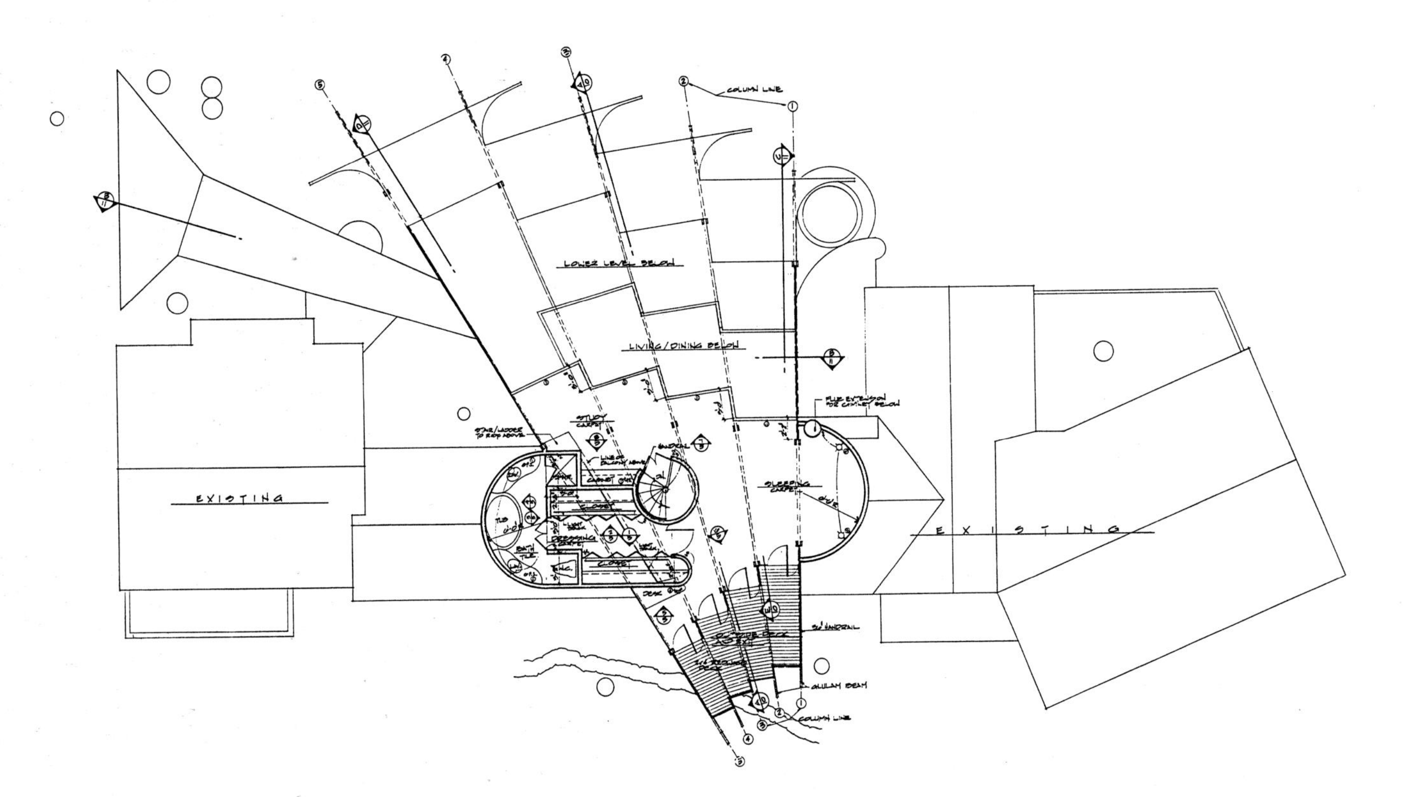

COLUMN LINE
LOWER LEVEL BELOW
LIVING/DINING BELOW
EXISTING
SLEEPING
HANDRAIL
DRESSING
CLOSET

Seymour house

Bart Prince

The Seymour residence, at Los Altos in California, was constructed fifty years ago as a summer hideaway. The successive owners have reformed and amplified it. The building was damaged by earthquakes, so it was decided to undertake a reform project.

The house is sited in a wood, surrounded by giant sequoias and oak trees. The relationship of the building with the wood, the idea of integrating it in these privileged surroundings, so that it forms part of the wood, is an initiative shared by the architect, Bart Prince, and the owners. «The Seymours liked the idea of a tree house, and wanted the greatest possible amount of natural light to enter all corners of the house», confessed Bart.

The reform carried out on the house is spectacular. However, it only affects the centre of the original building. The differences and the contrast between the two architects is enormous. Of course, the Seymours knew of the peculiar, expressionist forms of Bart Prince's works, and if they decided to contract him, it was, without doubt, because they intended to transform their discrete hideaway in the wood into a singular building, with inherent force. Obviously, the decision to conserve a large part of the house was not due to a cost problem, since the actual reform was not cheap. Why, then, didn't they build a completely new house?

On the following page, a general view of the rear part of the house. The Seymour residence is found surrounded by giant oaks and sequoias.

Below, aspect of the rear entrance to the house. The enormous glued, laminated, wood beams determine the form and aesthetics of the house.

The enclosures combine two different types of glass: transparent and translucent, depending on the degree of privacy required inside.

The whole project was based on this first decision. And for this reason we find out that the owners did not wish to carry out a rehabilitation or reform in a strict sense, but, neither did they want a new building, what they wanted was, for the oaks, the sequoias of the wood to finally penetrate the house.

The new structure bursts upon the centre of the house with a fan of glued, laminated, wood beams in the shape of enormous leaves, which go through the house from one end to the other.

The remodelling carried out by Bart Prince is divided into three floors, taking advantage of the slope of the ground. The building does not directly rest on the ground, but rather it is held on piles, forming a series of terraces. A small stream descends just in front of the house and crosses the property. The filiform beams support a curved, wooden roof finished on the outside with sequoia chips. All the vertical enclosures are made of glass. Bart Prince has combined transparent

A view of the main façade of the house. A small stream flows just in front of the dwelling. The house does not open directly onto the ground, but rather, through a series of terraces constructed on both sides.

On the previous page, detail of the enclosures. The bracing bars introduce new directions into the geometry of the building. Bart Prince has designed the steel carpentry as a skin which adapts itself to the structure of the house.

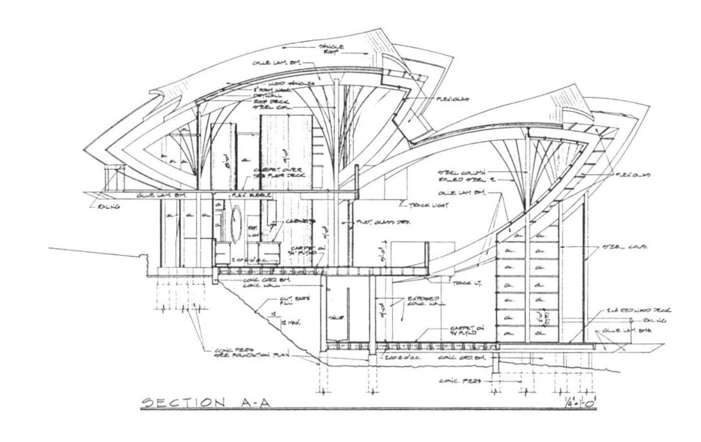

Transverse section

Both the exteriors and some of the interior walls are covered with wood chips in the form of twisting lines that confer an organic continuity to the whole.

panes with translucent ones in order to treat the light in different ways and to achieve different degrees of privacy and in relationship with the exterior vegetation. An attempt to multiply the possibilities of this material.

The roofs, the exterior walls and some of the interior walls are covered with a design of twisting lines of wood chips which wrap the surfaces, providing the whole with an organic continuity. In some places the lines follow a concentric circular path reminiscent of the cut trunk of a giant tree, perhaps the trunk of a sequoia.

The bedroom area and one of the living rooms were conserved from the original house.
The central part, where the oldest rooms were, was the part which had suffered most from the passage of time, so it was decided to build a new structure in this zone.

The main entrance is via a ramp, and halfway along it, a rotating door separates the exterior from the interior. The limits are imprecise. Bart Prince wished to construct a dwelling which formed part of the wood, so that the placing of the enclosures, even though of glass, was an uncomfortable decision. The architect finally decided to subordinate them to the structure, as if

On the following page, detail of the stairway. One of the elements with most impact is the great wheel with steel radials, anchored to one of the wooden beams above the stairway, which looks like a merry-go-round on the point of turning.

The structural beams of glued, laminated wood and the steel sections of the enclosures create a net which filters the vision of the exterior and transmits the feeling of being perched in the branches of a giant tree

a steel and glass web had been spun between the wooden beams.

On the ground floor can be found the kitchen, the chimney and the dining room, in relation to the rooms of the original house: the bedrooms, or a games-room. The same happens on the first floor, whose central part is occupied by the living room, where the sofas as well as the walls and floor have been covered in blue. On the upper floor is the master bedroom with a dressing room and a semi-circular bathroom which is illuminated by a round skylight. The master bedroom has an entrance via the rear terrace which allows an access independent from the rest of the house. The library was fitted out just above the bathroom in the highest part of the roof.

All the spaces in the house are interconnected since they are organised in terraces, where some fall away in form from the others creating a large area common to three floors. However, this space was not conceived as a vacuum, but as a network, formed by the wooden beams and the horizontal steel sections that support the glass panes; thus the interior of the house reminds one of the inside of a tree, the network of its branches. The separation of the different areas of the house is produced by the very same disposition of the spaces. The division of the house is produced principally in a vertical manner, that is, in section.

Even though the communion between nature and architecture achieved by Bart Prince in this project is almost complete, there is a still greater complicity within the dwelling, a stronger feeling, of refuge, of a marvellous hideaway in the most unpredictable place.

At night, the house is converted into a lamp in the heart of the wood. The interior illumination is projected onto the vegetation creating a phenomenon which is the opposite of that which is produced during the day.

The house has then become the soul of the wood. •

View of the main room.

On the elevation drawings, one can observe that the reform has only affected the central part of the house.

Aspect of the bedroom study, with the spiral staircase in the foreground and the library built over the bathroom. The majority of the surfaces are carpeted with the intention of providing greater quality to the interior.

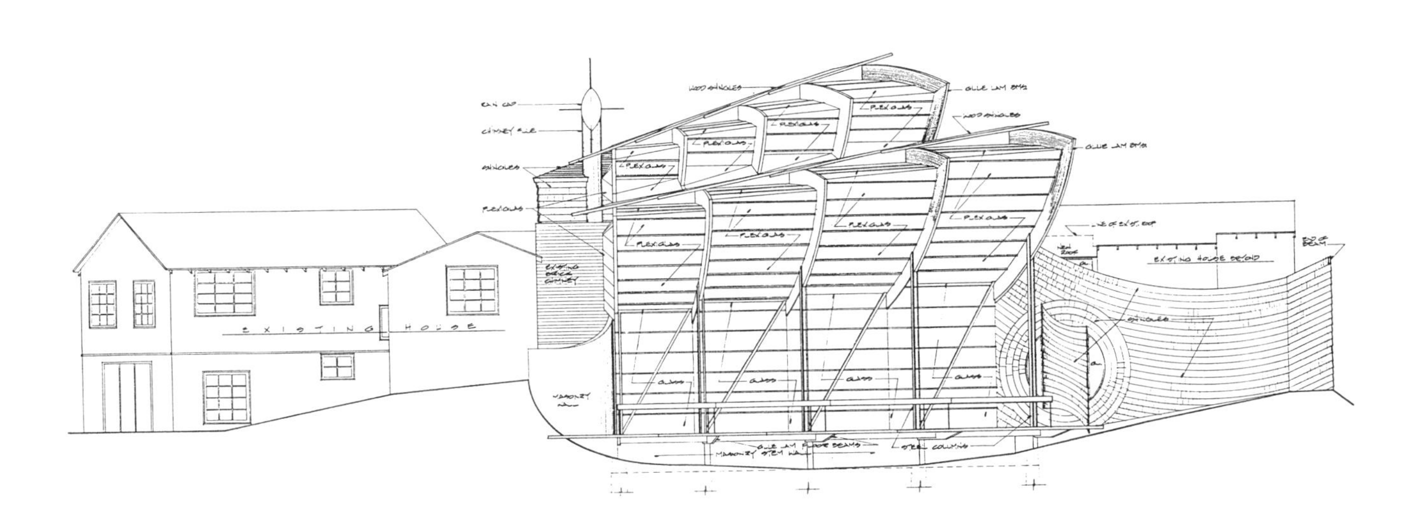

EXISTING HOUSE
WOOD SHINGLES
GLUE LAM BMS
PLEXIGLAS
GLASS
SHINGLES
MASONRY WALL
GLUE LAM FLOOR BEAMS
STEEL COLUMNS
EXISTING HOUSE BEYOND

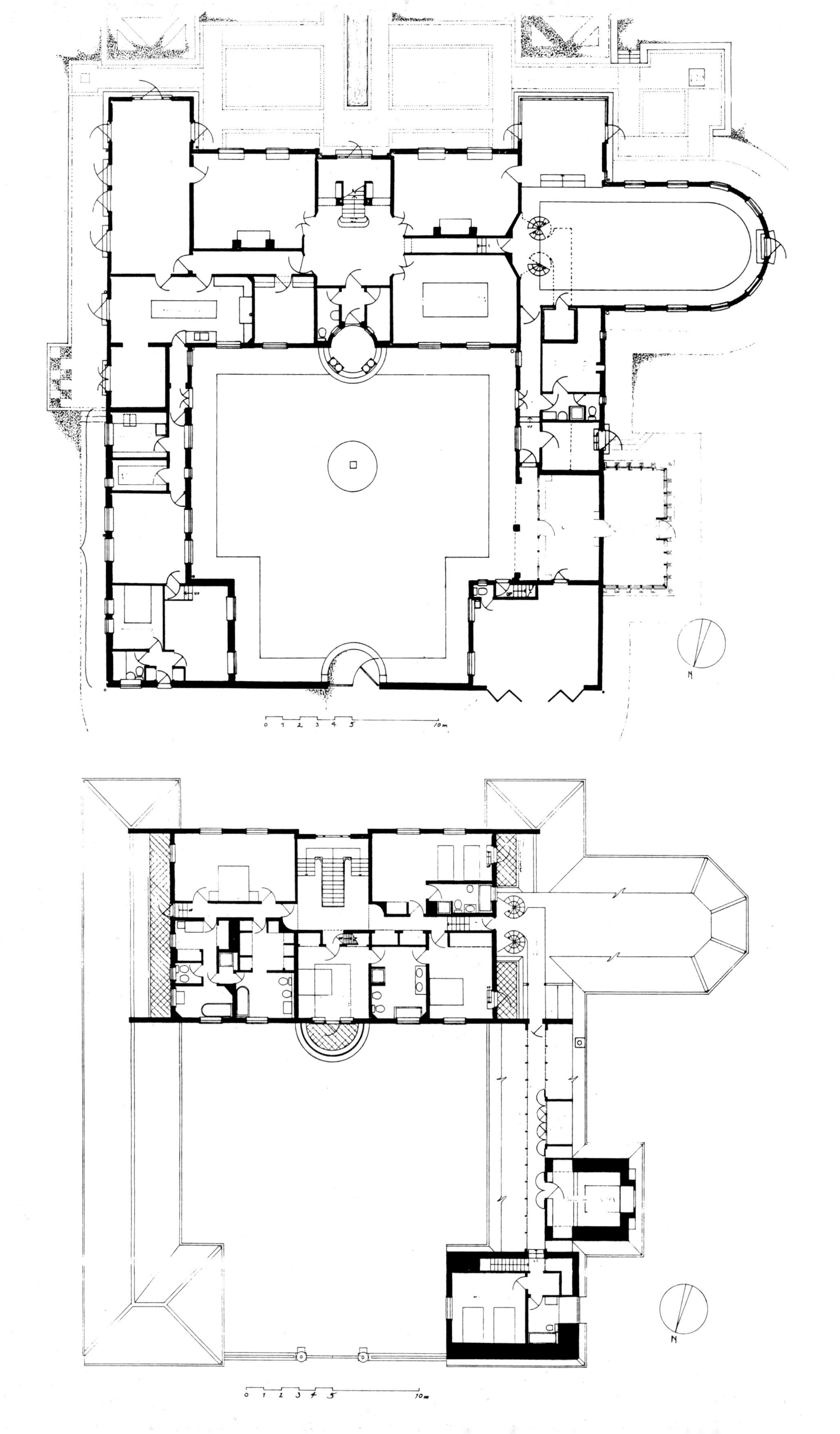
N
0 1 2 3 4 5 10m
N
0 1 2 3 4 5 10m

Plans of the ground and first floors.

Howe Green Manor

CZWG Architects

Beyond physical reality, exist certain landscapes which have a mythical existence. They are immediately-recognisable places, since the image we have of them comes before the actual place. The English countryside is one of these places. It is not simply a land, but a double landscape, both physical and cultural at the same time, weighed down with history and evocations. United with the topology, the vegetation, the specific peculiarities of each location, there is a simultaneous, inescapable image which cannot be removed because it is as real as the woods, as the climate or as the past.

Howe Green Manor is a huge, red brick mansion in Hertfordshire, in the green belt of the centre of England. Constructed in an extensive, undulating, green meadow surrounded by trees, the project's architects (Nick Campbell, Roger Zogolovitch, Rex Wilkinson, and Piers Gough, all of whom received degrees from the avant-garde Architectural Association School of London, at the end of the sixties) endeavoured to integrate the new residence, not only into its surroundings, placid and harmonious, but also into the architectonic history of the English countryside.

The house is constructed around a central patio which functions as a great exterior hall. The U-shaped plan is made up of a central building with two floors and two lateral wings that close the patio. Access is from the north, through a metal bar gate. From the north-facing, central patio the house unfolds like a fan, following the sun's path. Each room has a precise emplacement which is determined by the time of day when its use is most intense.

The entrance to the house is through a classic, semi-circular porch. Supported by two pairs of Doric columns which flank the entrance, it follows a composition inspired by the Venetian villas of Andrea Palladio. This small porch creates a hierarchic axis around which the main façade has been symmetrically structured.

The general volume of the house presents an almost pyramidal form. The residence grows gradually, like a small, artificial hill, from the lateral wings to the culminating point of the inclined tiled roof of the central building.

In the interior, the distribution is produced in a sequential manner. From the entrance, one arrives at a great hall, dominated by a flight of stairs that goes up to the first floor and which was thought of as a filtering element between the garden, extending behind the house, and the building. The sun's rays flood the space through a large, vertical window and allow one, no sooner across the threshold of the entrance, to catch a glimpse of the existence of this exuberant, meridional garden.

In the rectangular hall, the corners are cut at an angle to allow the positioning of four symmetrical doors, through which access is made to the principal rooms of the house: two identical living rooms, with views onto the south garden, on both sides of the hall, and, on the north façade, a billiard room and a study, which is reached by crossing the corridor which ends in the dining room, a large, long room in the southeast vertex of the building.

The service rooms are in the east wing: the kitchen, a small adjacent room, for breakfasting in the early morning sun, which has direct access to the east garden, the pantry and the servants quarters, with a private entrance from the street.

The west wing is organised around a large, indoor swimming pool in a round-topped pavilion which juts out into the west garden. A band of

A view of the south façade from the south garden. On both sides of the central building, the two lateral wings are highlighted by the two pavilions on a single floor corresponding to the dining room and the summer house next to the swimming pool. Small terraces, with direct access to the bedrooms on the first floor, are hidden above these pavilions. The volumetric composition has a pyramidal character, crowned by a hipped, tiled roof and the chimney towers in each of the vertices.

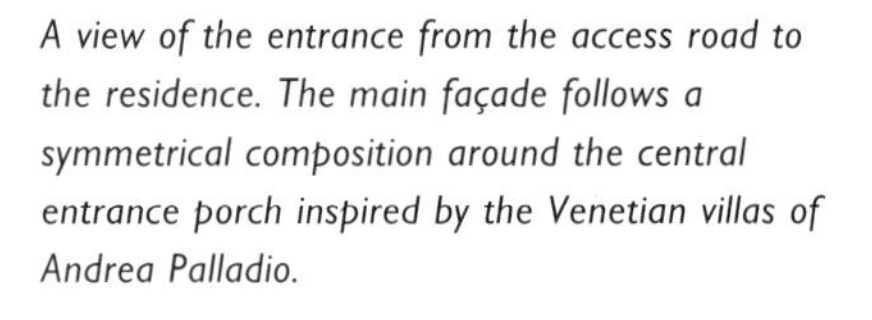

A view of the entrance from the access road to the residence. The main façade follows a symmetrical composition around the central entrance porch inspired by the Venetian villas of Andrea Palladio.

perimeter windows let the afternoon sun's rays into the room which are reflected from the surface of the water and inundate the walls with shadows in movement to accompany a late bathe. On both sides of the swimming pool can be found some of the other rooms such as the gymnasium, the boiler room, the changing room and the sauna, all directly linked. A small summer house has also been constructed to unite the swimming pool and the garden.

In the extreme north of the wing, next to the residence's entrance, is the garage with direct access to the street and also a small independent office.

The upper floor is completely occupied by the bedrooms and their corresponding dressing rooms and bathrooms. A passage between closets joins the central group of bedrooms with two others at the far end of the west wing which have direct access from the central patio by an independent stairway. The passage forms a small balcony above the swimming pool. Two metal spiral staircases allow immediate access to the swimming pool from the bedrooms.

The taste for detail, for the exquisite design of a specific element, such as an eclectic window, between Gothic and oriental, a metal stairway with a proto-industrial aspect or some interior finish inspired by Rushkin and the arts and crafts movement: all evidence that, behind the general homogeneous image of the residence lies a second level, on a lesser scale, in which the project work is equally important. The architecture at this level operates with a different kind of material, since they are no longer just walls or roofs, but also the capacity to express, through the spaces, evocations, feelings and associated emotions. Thus, the architect, thanks to the construction of certain images taken from the collective imagination or from yearning people, has the possibility to construct the domestic spaces as a prolongation of the feelings of those who inhabit them.

The architecture does not convert itself into its own purpose, it does not look for the spectacle of a novel balancing act, nor does it unfold a chain of fluid spaces, rather that each room is conceived as a scene, full of images and associations.

The proliferation of places which enclose a particular world, the homogeneous treatment of the exterior parameters, the brick walls as well as the tiled roof, recover the colour of the earth and the spatial distribution, searching for the best orientation, causes the house to transcend its condition of a simple, architectonic object placed on the landscape, to become part of it and to convert itself into land. ●

On the following page, details of the east wing pavilions. The glass conservatory is the result of a later intervention.

The interior of the swimming pool, under the two spiral staircases. The reflections on the water duplicate the perimeter windows.

Daphne Gough was responsible for the interior design of the children's rumpus room, which fits in well with the main features of the house. The circular window, inspired by the Taoist yin-yang sign, reflects the taste for introducing some exotic reference into the details

Below, the interior aspect of the conservatory. The pale tones and the roll-up curtains, together with the unpolished, ceramic-tiled paving, reproduce a warm, tranquil atmosphere.

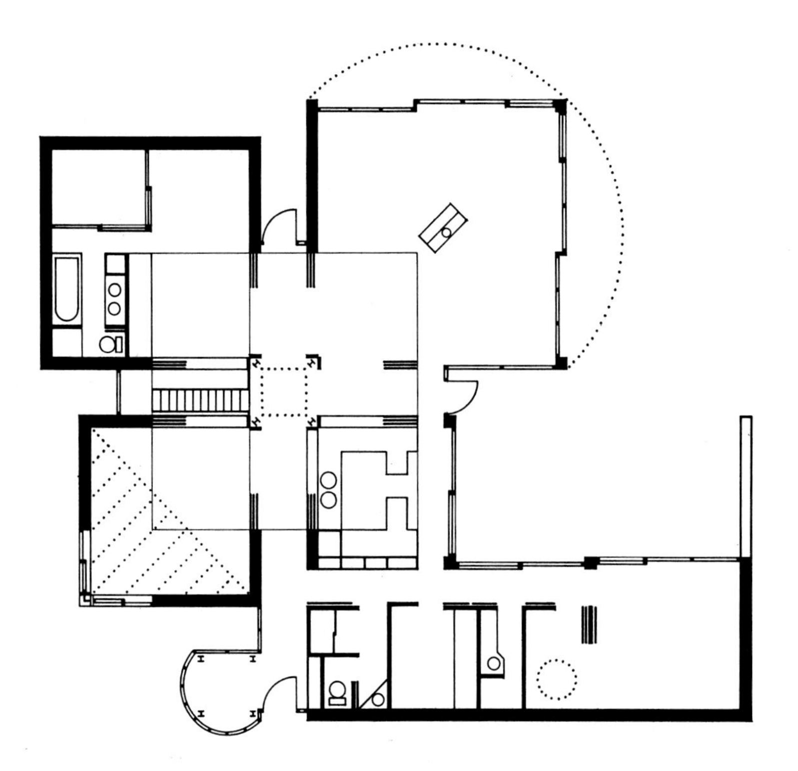

Main floor plan.

Van Veelen house

Cees Dam & Partners

Closed, introverted spaces exist in the Van Veelen house, there are also rooms which are completely open to the exterior, that seem to form part of the wood. The distribution of the rooms and the corridors that unite the house from one extreme to the other, cross, drawing a line of perpendicular axes. The walls shift with the imprecise geometry of neoplastic compositions, and yet, beyond this apparent orthogonality, a whole range of visual connections cross the spaces diagonally and unite the opposite corners. Each space is an independent unit and, at the same time, the limits which separate them, may experiment certain transformations that convert them into corners or into the references of a larger space.

By moments, one would say that the house is organised based on a inexistent structure of partitions which displace themselves forming temporary distributions that continually vary; but, paradoxically, there are walls constructed from concrete blocks that form almost perfect squares.

From the wood, the house appears to have a single floor and its rooms are eventfully scattered, and, from the other side, the picture is almost the opposite, that of a house with two floors, with perfectly formed limits. On one façade, the composition is generated as a combination of glass planes and solid surfaces, while on the opposite, it is produced as a dialogue between clearly defined

The narrow stone-flagged path which leads up to the glass entrance. The study's skylight is the only inclined roof of the residence.

At the rear of the house, the relation between the interior and the exterior is complete. The paving continues from one side to the other of the great windows. A sculpture in the living room reminds one of the exterior forms of vegetation.

A view of the rear of the house from the wood. The roof is constructed on different levels. The study's skylight and the one which illuminates the central point where the interior corridors cross, jut out from the surface.

volumes and narrow openings which are cut out of the walls.

Even though we recognise resources and references of the masters of modern architecture, details which remind us of Mies van der Rohe, Arne Jacobsen, Louis Khan, Frank Lloyd Wright, de Stijl or Aldo van Eyck, nothing here turns out to be paradigmatic, nor exemplary, they do not even make up repetitions or references, everything is concrete and near, everything appears to be in perfect communion with its surroundings and to be produced in a necessary manner

The floor of the house is structured on the basis of two perpendicular corridors. In each one of the resulting quadrants is placed a determined area of the house: the living room, the master bedroom, a study and an area for guests. The first three are perfect squares: the living room measures 7 x 7 metres, the bedroom 6 x 6 and the study 5 x 5, so that following an anticlockwise direction, each room diminishes a metre per side.

The central corner of each of these rooms is formed from sliding partitions that allow them to be completely isolated, or to integrate them into a

An aspect of the living room porch. The curtain allows the play with transparencies and with visual lines across the patio.

On the following page, above, the front façade has a great solidness. The volumetric conception plays with the composition of solid bodies, with hardly any openings. On the other hand, the slope of the ground permits the location of the car park on an inferior half-buried floor.

On the following page, below, an aspect of the façade of the guests' section. The curtains and the sliding partitions permit an almost total independence.

single space that comprises them all.

The fourth quadrant has a different form. Next to the spot where the two corridors cross, the geometric centre, indicated by a skylight, the kitchen is thought of as the real centre of the house, the place around which life develops, a similar function to the chimneys in the prairie houses of Wright. In a certain way, this slight displacement of the centre seems to originate the internal movement of the house. The guest area, a long passageway, is therefore somewhat displaced, so that, although the rooms are integrated into the same building, they can enjoy a certain independence.

Although all the main rooms of the house are on the same floor, the slight slope of the ground has enabled Cees Dam to situate the car park on a half-buried floor.

The house relates itself with its surroundings in two completely distinct forms. Although the façade of two floors with access for cars is based on two precise volumes, separated by an intermediate glass section, and with very narrow openings, as the ground rises, the volumetric conception of the façade disappears, the forms articulate like walls with panes of glass which join them and close the interior space. Moreover, the rear and more hidden side of the house, is conceived as an exterior patio, closed by both the building and the pre-existing trees, onto which open the communal rooms of the house: the living room, the kitchen and also the guest area.

The living room is the space which is most open to the exterior of the residence. A circular porch, circumscribed on the volume of the room, protects it from the sun's rays. The paving, grey

On the following page, above, a view of the living room. Grey tones dominate the interior.

-On the following page, below, detail of the metal chimney, which occupies a central position in the room.

The sliding partition walls, used to define the space according to the whims of the occupants, is a device which is used throughout the house.

ceramic tiles, is continuous between the interior and the exterior. The interior is organised in different areas around a metal chimney situated in the centre of the room.

All the elements of furniture are exclusive models from some of the most well-known modern designers and architects, such as, Le Corbusier or Gerrit Rietvel.

The master bedroom is a completely introverted room, without any exterior windows. Cees Dam has designed a small interior patio which allows the space to be illuminated and, at the same time, resolves the relationship between the bathroom and the bedroom. A decision which reminds one of the houses with patios projected by Mies van der Rohe. In spite of this conception of the house as a fluid space with overlapping rooms, the corridors constitute a constant reference. There is a glass door at each extreme of the corridors which connects with the exterior, so that if one enters by the main door or by any of the garden doors, one can immediately see the other exit. This produces the sensation that the house is the intermediate space, not the place where one comes to rest at the end of each working day and from where one starts again each morning, but simply a small, private space in the never-ending road, protected from the climate, a small inhabited bend in the wood. •

The kitchen, designed by Cees Dam, is very sophisticated. It has a totally white ceiling and the furniture and fittings are black-veined imitation marble.

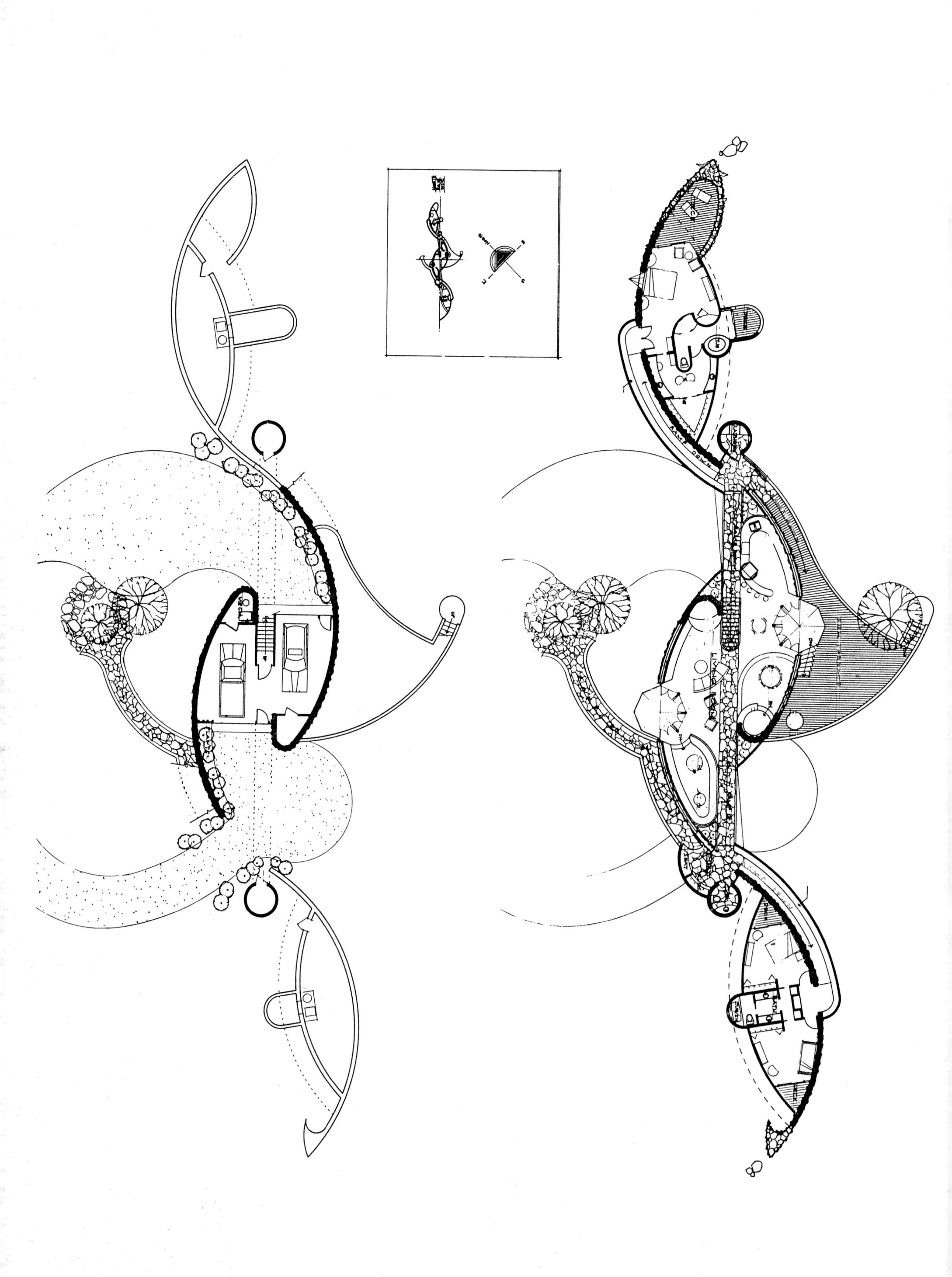

Bart Prince

In this house in Sun Valley, Idaho, the American architect, Bart Prince, has lifted architecture to new heights. It is not just that the undulating walls, the curved roofs, the twisting forms and the earthy colours integrate into the countryside with uncommon wisdom, they are also confused with the hills and they adapt to the outlines which have been imposed by the wind during centuries, no, it is not just this. Bart Prince is able to push architecture to more complex sensations. The house in Sun Valley has rescued the mystery of the plains, its sleeping strength, from the silence and apparent tranquillity.

Bart Prince is not inspired by the typical houses of the region, in the traditional construction methods, in the commonplace techniques, in the use of wood or of tree trunks, his reconciliation with the terrain is of another kind, which has nothing in common with the accustomed architectural references.

From the nearby hills, the house appears more like a desert animal, an imitation reptile that moves forward through the valley with extreme parsimony, slowed down by the sun and the heat released by the earth and yet, stalking, possessed of an unexpected agility, capable of unleashing an extraordinary, contained force in a single, instant gesture, a whiplash, in which it engulfs an insect, that does not have the time to feel even a shiver, only a moment later the valley returns to its peaceful state once again.

Above, detail of the central skylight. The displacement of the two equal, curved beams produces a movement of torsion in the plane formed by the transversal wooden beams and the panes of glass.

A view from the window over the headrest in the master bedroom. In this element can be found the architect's efforts to subordinate the construction details to the formal expression of the building.

The owner of this house has another dwelling in the nearby locality of Bliss, designed by Frank Lloyd Wright, the architect whose work had a great influence on the architecture of Bart Prince. His concept was to construct a dwelling with architectonic value and an intrinsic attractiveness, as a lure for later renting or selling to one of the many visitors who wish to rest during some period of the year in this region. The house is sited in extensive grounds, dry, without trees or buildings, without any other reference than the hills close to the dwelling and the very silence, absence.

The building structure is based on two walls in the form of an elongated "S" which overlap. In fact, the floor describes an inverted symmetry with respect to a central axis. The architect took advantage of the concavities of the curved layout to construct the different dependencies. In this way, the house is divided into three distinct areas, which, in plan, have the form of a leaf.

In the central block, the largest of the three, with two floors, is situated the garage on the ground floor and the communal rooms, the living room, the dining room and the kitchen are on the first floor. In each one of the lateral buildings are the bedrooms, the master double bedroom is in one of them and in the other are two single bedrooms. These blocks are placed on a lower level with respect to the central block, so that it is necessary to go down ramps to get to the bedrooms from the living room. However, they are not at ground level, but somewhat higher, so that their respective, half-buried ground floors can be used as store-rooms.

Bart Prince has been able to make the different areas of the house independent, thanks to this unusual distribution of the rooms. An elongation of the normal connections has been produced and the distances covered acquire a greater role, not only on the plan, but also within the general volume of the building.

The living space is divided by a central passage, paved with irregular, grey stone, in contrast to the rest of the house which has parquet

Even though the house achieves a perfect integration with the countryside, its form is not homogeneous since it is composed of distinct elements and materials.

The south-east aspect of the house. In spite of the irregular plan shape, the house has a basically lineal character.

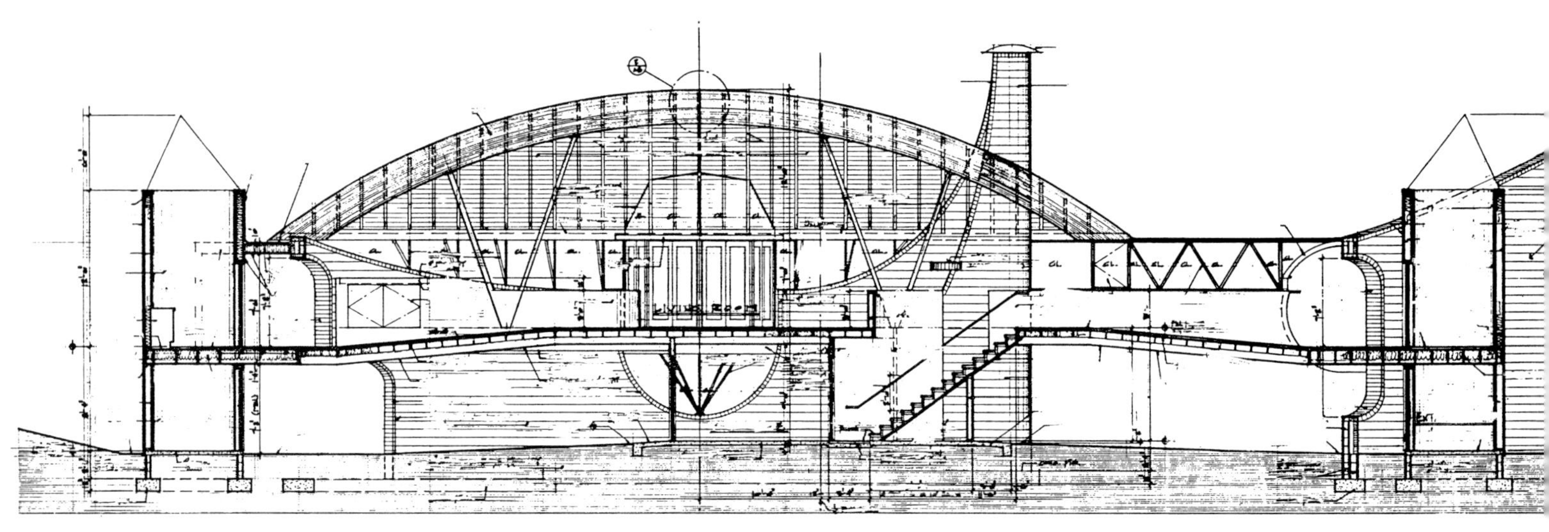

From the living room one can see the people who cross the passageway in an image which places them into the landscape.

On the left, a partial view of the living room. The sliding windows along the whole of the façade and the zenithal skylight, combined with the chosen material, produce the impression of being inside the landscape.

Longitudinal section.

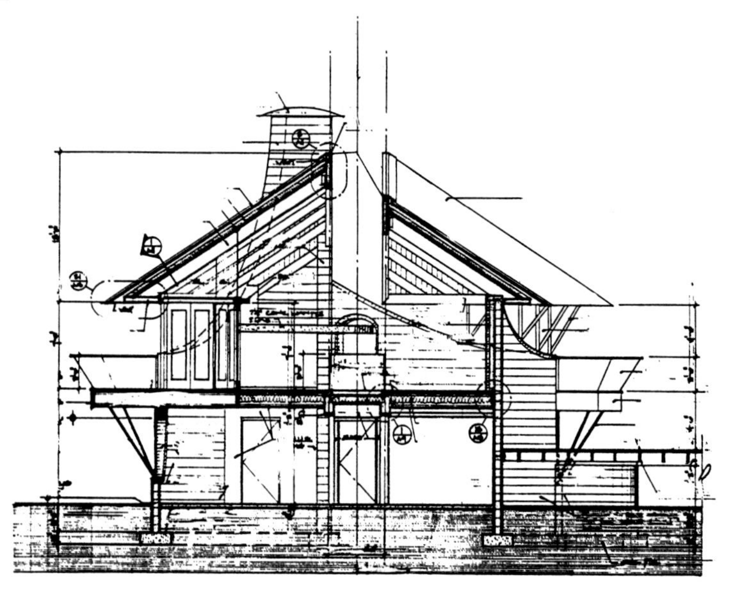

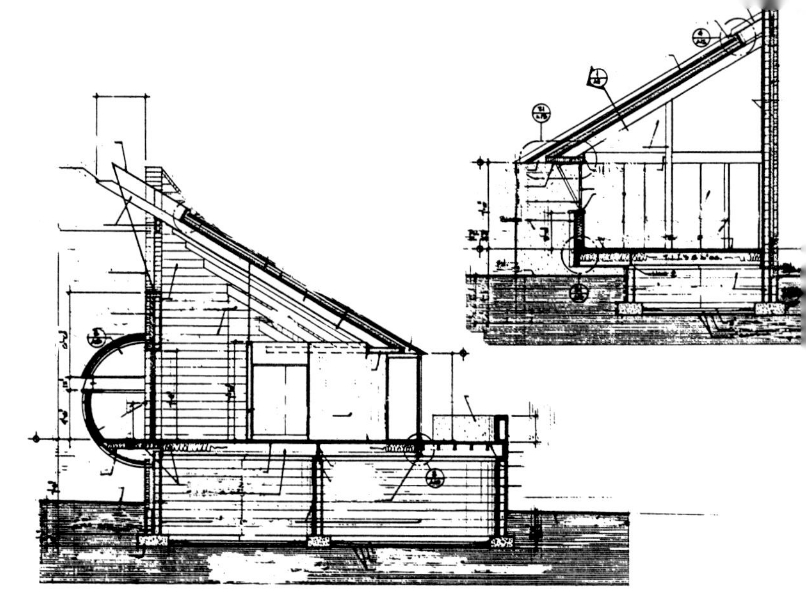

Transverse sections.

or is carpeted. This central corridor, with the access stairs to the garage, is illuminated by a long skylight. The two curved roofs which cover each one of these sides of the drawing room are interrupted in the central section, leaving an open strip between two curved, wooden beams, and slightly displaced on the direction of their axes. In this way, the transverse beams, which unite the two arches and support the glass panes of the skylight, make up a twisted fillet which stamps the building with tension and dynamism.

This movement is prolonged through the ramps which go from the living room to the bedrooms, made like a semi-spherical tube which adapts itself to the curve of the façade. In this way, the dynamism of the plan is perfectly visible, not only in the exterior aspect of the building, but also in the explicit understanding of the house through its interior passageways.

The form of each one of the rooms, the kitchen as well as the bedrooms, the terraces or the bathrooms, adapt themselves to the general curves of the building, a sequential succession of spaces and inherent movement from which issues the spirit of the dwelling. The furniture must adapt itself to the architecture; the design of a table or the inclusion of a circular bench, are directly linked to the whole, so that each detail finds its explanation in the others and permits the association of a precise rhythm to the spaces. Moreover, in some cases, such as in the kitchen or the distribution of the bathrooms, the arrangement of the pieces or of the sanitary fittings is carefully chosen, so that the inclusion of each element

A dramatic, twisting skylight joins these roof forms above the central passageway which separates the living and entertainment areas from the kitchen and dining areas.
In some details, one can appreciate the interest that Bart Prince has for movements, which like Art Nouveau, it is currently difficult for them to be taken as reference.

Detail of the wooden structure which supports the arches of the roof.

organises its surrounding space, separates the distinct areas of the rooms and allows a gradual access to the more intimate places.

But, not only does the general profile or the internal structure of the house adapt themselves to their surroundings, to the gentle curves of the hills, to the wind, and to the harsh sun of the plains; but also to the texture and colours of the building, reproducing the earthy tones and the dryness of the territory. And if the aspect of the building transmits the idea of great internal coherence, the materials used are so different, stone, tile, plaster and wood; because Bart Prince wanted to unfold all the possibilities of the empty, colourless terrain of Sun Valley through the use of different textures, lustre and tones.

The encounters between the distinct elements introduced an added complexity, a parallel tension which reveals the formal bid of the project. The gently twisting roofs, the curved walls which hug the house, the stairs and the ramps, they disturb the silence with the force of a hunting reptile. •

Some of the exterior materials are used in the interior, such as stone, or even the rounded edges which introduce references to the landscape.

On the following page, detail of the kitchen, perfectly illuminated with natural light. The furniture must adapt itself to the curved forms of the building.

On the right, a view of the corridor which crosses the living room from the end of the access ramp to the bedrooms.

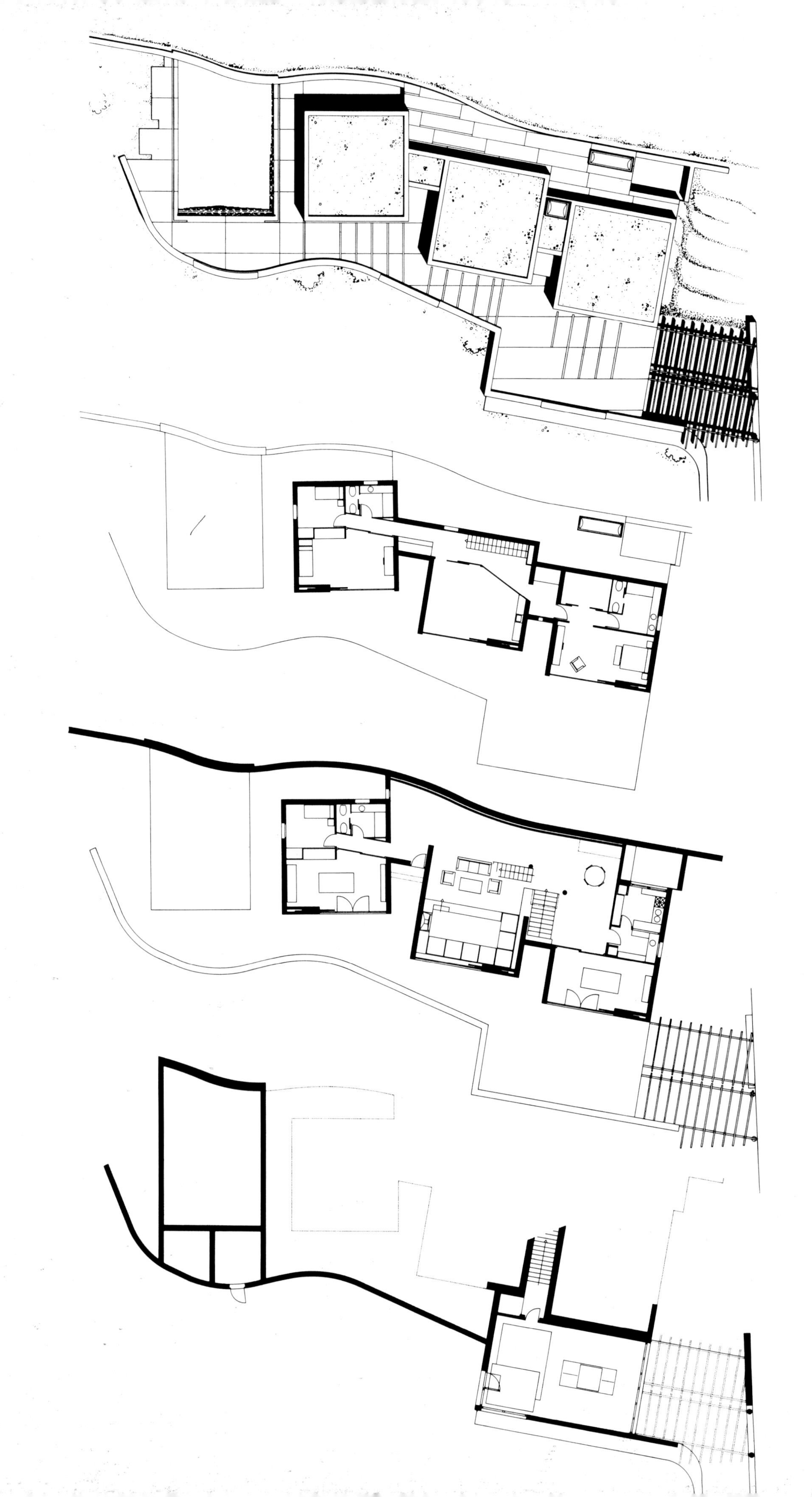

Plans.

Hidalgo house

Jordi Garcés and Enric Sòria

This single-family dwelling is an excellent creative project carried out by two architects from Barcelona, Jordi Garcés and Enric Sòria. The formal design of the structure is an abstract set of three cubes on a steeply-sloping site in Alella on the Catalan coast. This original piece of architecture won the 1987 FAD prize.

The Hidalgo House was built on a 450 m^2 site stretching out from east to west, bordered on the southern side by a steep slope going down to the road. Thanks to its considerably elevated location the structure is well placed to receive sunlight, and commands a marvellous view over the sea.

Taking advantage of the topographical features of the site the two architects carried out an extremely creative project based on the simplest of geometric lines. Thus the single-family dwelling was structured from the premise of an abstract set of three cubic units and three large windows interrelated by the variable rhythm of their respective positions. Viewed from the exterior the house is a huge, sober and uniform structure, since all its exterior walls are smooth, grey rendered surfaces.

In the three polyhedrons, the main sea-facing elevation contains an enormous rectangular metal-framed window divided into large square panes.

These openings stretch from the floor on the first level to the ceiling on the second level in a single sweep. Their huge size means that they play

a major role in the configuration of the building. They are also fundamental features in that they allow sunlight to penetrate all interior areas, thus creating a pleasant warm atmosphere inside the house.

The other elevations are practically closed off, although there are a number of narrow, rectangular wooden windows on other planes in contrast to the huge main windows.

The swimming pool is located at the west of the property. It is rectangular, thereby matching the cubes of the basic construction. This shape is not, however, completely regular, since the containing wall which surrounds it on one side curves around in a wavy line.

The rigid exterior geometry is less marked inside the house, where the space is continuous and fluid. However, since the windows on the main elevations correspond to the various planes, inside the building the triplecube concept of this original composition can be observed.

General view. The hidalgo house is organised into three equal cubes with two floors, some turned with respect to the others, as in the compositions of Kasimir Malevitch. In the foreground is an aspect of the garage.

On the following page, a lateral view of the house, with the swimming pool in the foreground. The terrain presented a steep slope so the house had to be built between two retaining walls.

The house is integrated into the minimalist current. The exterior aspect is one of great austerity. The walls have simply been left whitewashed.
The windows are two storeys high.

A general view of the living and dining rooms. Although the volumes are clearly differentiated from the exterior, in the interior, they succeed each other in a continuous manner.

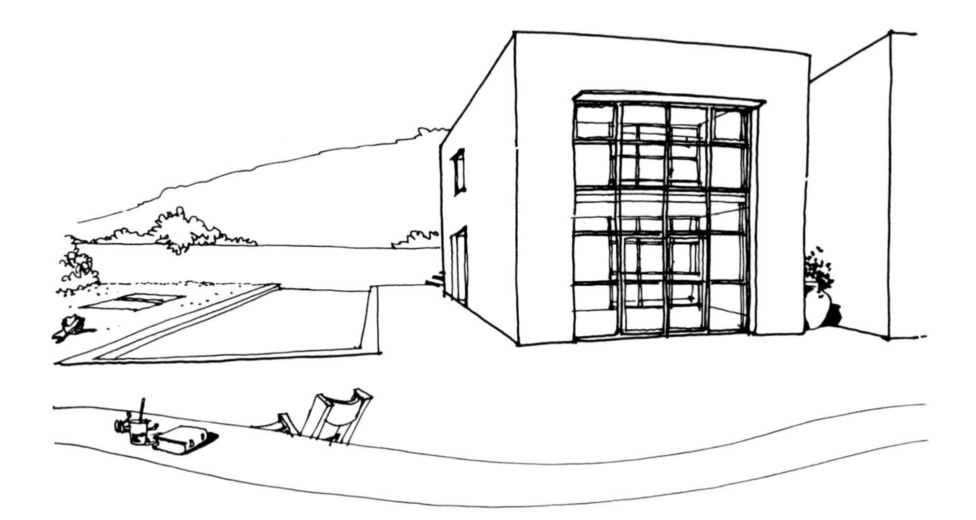

Inside this unusual structure, the traditional layout of a modern dwelling has been strictly observed. The house is laid out on two upper floors and a ground floor providing access.

While on the upper level the architects housed the more private rooms, the main floor below contains the day areas and communal zones. There are three bedrooms and two fully- equipped bathrooms on the second floor, and a service bedroom complete with bathroom, as well as the lounge, dining room, office and kitchen on the first floor.

Once again the joint efforts of Jordi Garcés and Enric Sòria have produced a curious masterpiece. The exterior rigidity of these three cubes dominated by large windows contrast with the spatial fluidness of the interior, making the Hidalgo House an ambivalent modern construction independent of the surrounding countryside. ●

Detail of the living room. The same minimalist spirit of the exterior finishes is repeated in the selection of the furniture. The living area has been resolved by the collocation of a set of geometric cushions.

The columns and the stairway have been designed with a great purity of form. Each element has its own identity. The polished surfaces accentuate the contrast of colours and shadows.

An aspect of one of the corridors of the upper floor. The passageway is illuminated through translucent doors and windows.

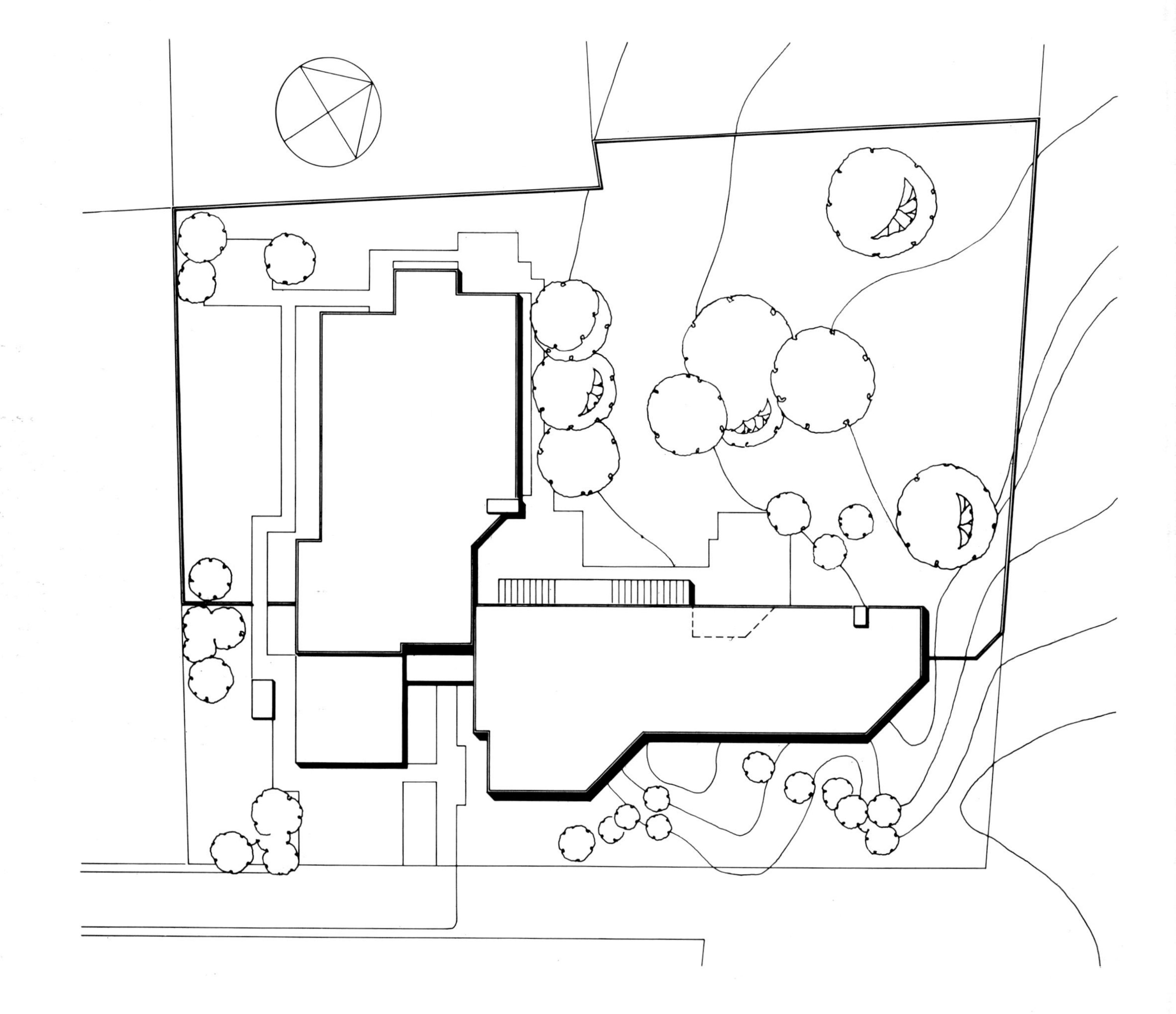

General plan of the house.

House in Hämeelinna

Jukka Siren

The Finnish architect Jukka Siren designed this house to meet the challenge of creating a series of rooms and spaces capable of providing all the comforts and amenities required by the inhabitants, while fulfilling the particular functions necessary in a home in the generally adverse climate of this country.

This single-family dwelling in Hämeenlinna, Finland, is built at the end of a residential street close to Hattelmala hill. The house is moulded to the sloping site, and fits in effortlessly with the natural features of the terrain, surrounded by abundant, flourishing vegetation and splendid views.

A path from the street leads to an outdoor play area on the east side. The wall surrounding the property forms a kind of patio garden which has been left in a natural state: a scattering of rocks and pine trees. The building is laid out on a L-shaped floor plan made up of two separate wings connected by the vertex where they join at right angles. The two-storey residential wing separates the back garden from the street. Inside the house, on the ground floor, the dining room, kitchen, living area and library are laid out in a line on slightly different levels according to the slope of the land, and are linked by a few steps.
The dining room and living room are connected

through a large square opening in the partition wall between them.

All these rooms open onto the garden through a glass wall forming one of the facades.

The upper floor includes the bedrooms and an adjoining full-length covered deck which affords a view of the garden and overlooks the single-storey northwest wing. This wing, adjoining the main house, contains the sauna, relaxation area, swimming pool, storeroom, garage and other auxiliary service areas.

The architect's chief aim was to achieve spatial continuity in an interior free of non-essential physical barriers. The entire ground floor is a single enormous space which is the hub of the life of the family. We must remember that the house is in Finland, and for at least six or seven months of the year the occupants spend many hours

View of the entrance to the house. The house has few openings to the street. However, it is completely open to the garden full of huge trees at the rear.

The house is perfectly adapted to the terrain. The architect has not only respected the existing trees but has also adapted the building to the abrupt topography, leaving a small front garden where the profile of the house dialogues with the rocks.

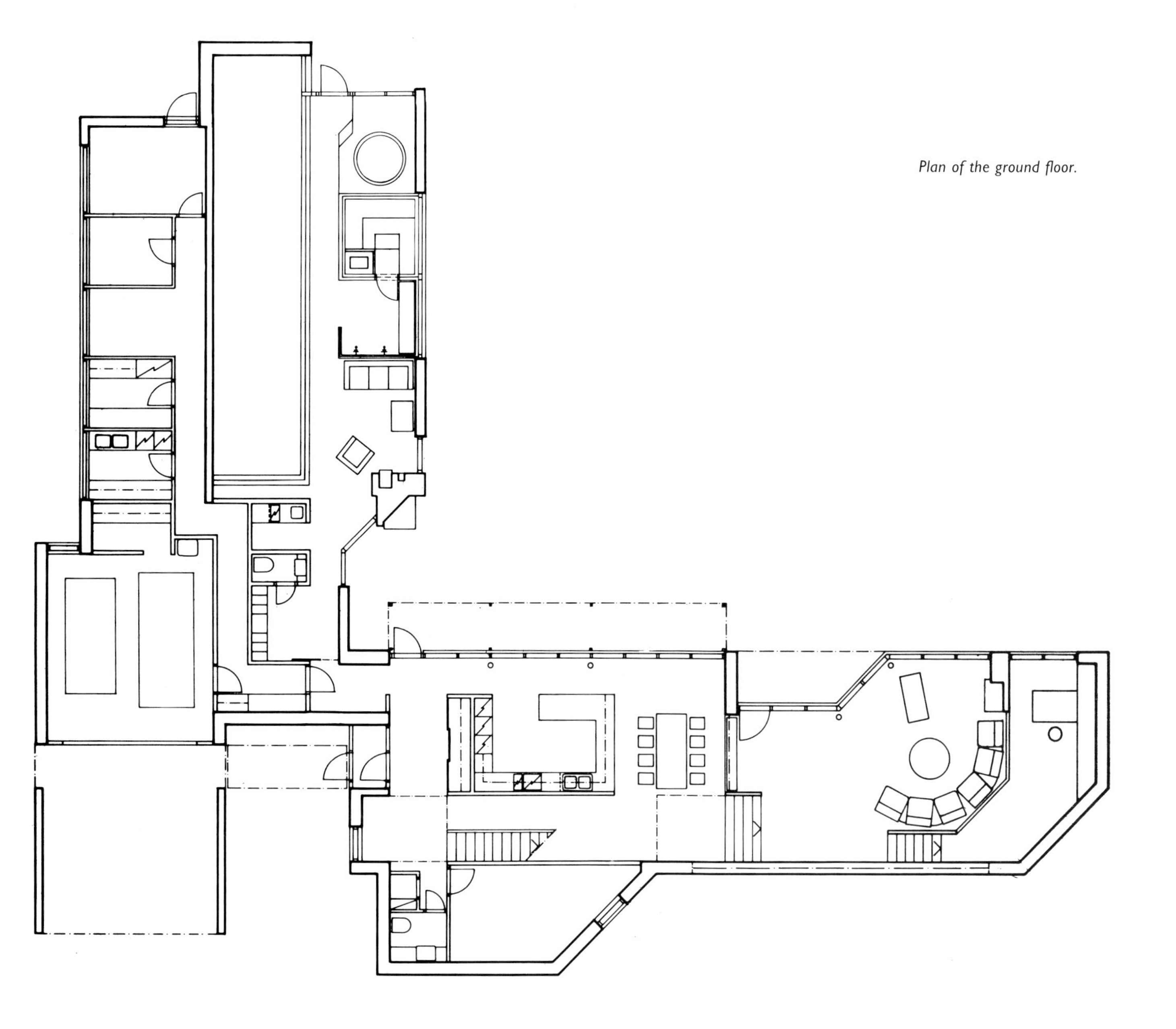

Plan of the ground floor.

indoors owing to the freezing, inclement weather. The elimination of any nonessential partition walls makes it easier for the different members of the family to be together, although they may be involved in different activities. The rooms are distinguished from one another by the different levels, and this separation is emphasised by the difference in the materials used. The living room and library floors and ceilings are finished in wood, for example, while the kitchen and dining room have tiled floors and white plastered ceilings. Function is therefore subordinate to the design, and also to the stepped structure of the house.

The manner in which this dwelling confronts the sun is more complex than a person from other latitudes would think. The house is not orientated to the south. The septentrional sun is too weak

Detail of the rear terraces. Although the house is in a clearly recognisable L-shape, the small offsets and the terraces transform the perimeter into an organic profile that completely integrates itself into the surrounding nature.

The visual relationship between the exuberant garden and the living room, improved by the large glass surfaces, make winter days more bearable when it is almost impossible to go outside. Longitudinal section through the living room.

and is absent during many months of the year. The heating of the house is entrusted to machines. But, above all, on many occasions the sun is too low and, therefore, the horizontal rays are bothersome. For this reason, the windows which are orientated towards the morning sun are narrow, so that the sun enters the house in the form of precise, almost tangible beams, with the force of a revelation. It is more important to manifest and celebrate the appearance of the sun,

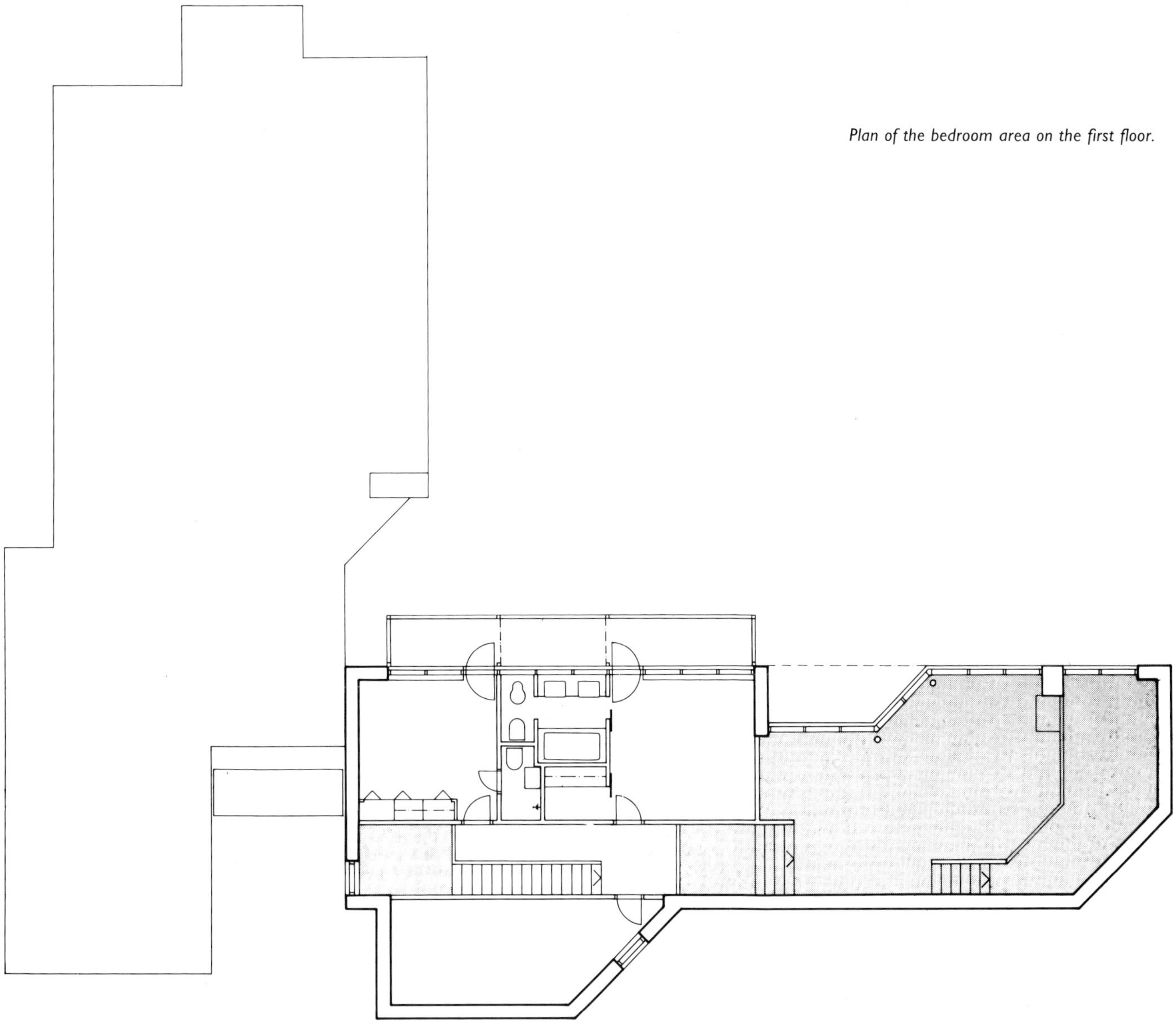

Plan of the bedroom area on the first floor.

than to benefit from its low calorific capacity. The opposite façade, open to the interior garden is orientated towards the more intense afternoon sun. It is good that it completely penetrates the house, but it must be filtered.

The swimming pool is located inside the house, where the temperature can be artificially controlled. With these factors in mind the architect protected the building from the elements by constructing a system of partially covered terraces and deep porches, and by fitting the main parts of the house with lattice screens which discharge this function perfectly. In addition, the windows and doors are fitted with roll-up shutters on the outside, and delicate transparent white curtains inside. This system provides complete control of the environment, which can be regulated according to the requirements of the occupants whatever the climatological conditions. For the same reasons, the pool is located inside the house where the temperature can be artificially controlled.

This does not mean, however, that the architect wished to isolate the building from the surrounding landscape. On the contrary, the floor-to-ceiling glass wall enclosing one side of the ground floor brings the interior into close contact with nature. The rooms are inundated with morning sunlight bringing in the colour and freshness of the outdoors. As if this were not enough, a large number of plants have been used to decorate the rooms. In fact, the very structure of the house in the form of an L seems to embrace the surrounding greenery.

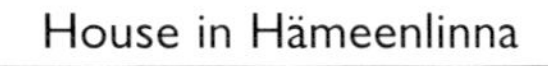

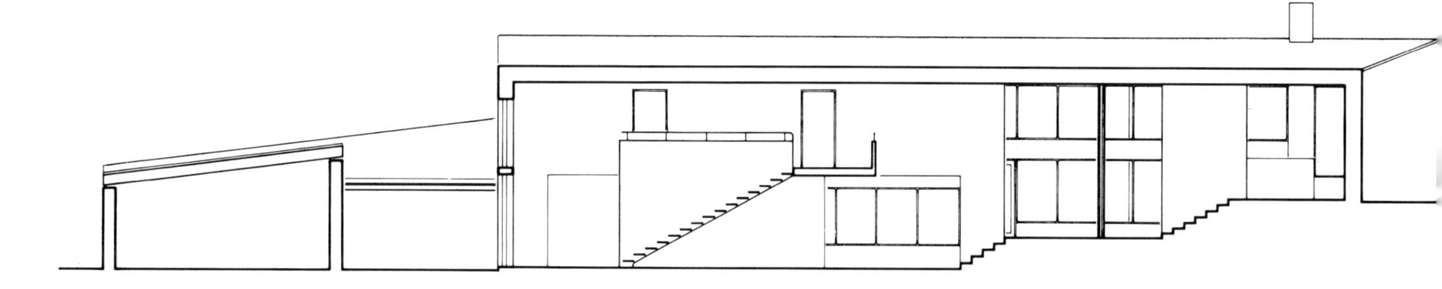

The interior is though of as a unique space along the complete length of a stepped corridor. Each area occupies an independent space, covered and paved with different materials, although maintaining a visual continuity with the whole.

On the previous page, a general view of the northwest façade. The exterior finishes combine brick, wood and metal, all painted white. Among the trees, moulded as if it were a snow-covered mountain, the house seems to belong to the landscape.

As for the choice of materials, the facades are a combination of limestone bricks, wood and steel, all painted white, giving the entire composition a clean, sharp outline. The roof is made of metal sheeting, clear polycarbonate and polished reinforced glass. Inside the house, birchwood ceilings were used to soundproof the structure, and beech wood, marble and ceramic tiles were used for the floors.

His deep understanding of the climatological conditions of his native land and his love for its vegetation and landscape led this Finnish architect to create a house where the spatial continuity confers great breadth and room for movement on all the rooms in this open-plan design which favours family life and social relations, especially during the harshest seasons of the year. Thus, the house is a refuge where the owners can enjoy the privileged setting, and at the same time have all the comforts and amenities of a modern home in this sometimes bleak and remote setting. •

A view of the room with the swimming pool. Leisure must be incorporated into the house, since this is where the Finns spend the greater part of their free time.

A partial view of the living room. The curtains filter the sun's rays. The different heights of the spaces introduces a subtle hierarchical relationship.

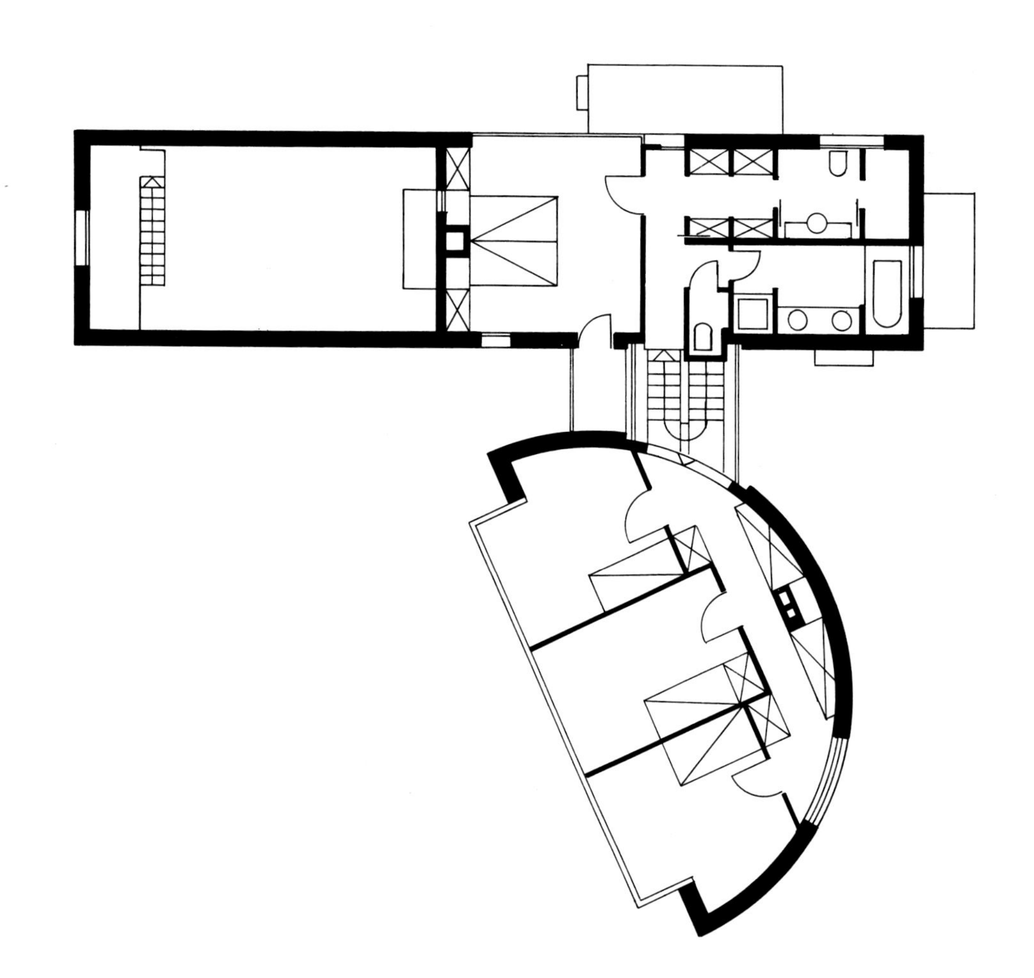

House in Taunus

On the outskirts of Taunus, near Frankfurt, on a small hill which rises from among huge cedars, is the house designed by the German architect, Christoph H. Mäckler, a dwelling thought out from duality. The architect wished to put forth a dialogue between opposites, designing two completely different buildings which would introduce an additional dynamism into the project.

To an orthogonal building, with the floor plan in an L-shape, was fitted a semi-circular tower. The shape, the relationship with the surroundings, the colour, the finishes, the materials, ... everything about them is different. But, it is more than this, they oppose each other.

The L-shaped building moulds itself to the terrain. It is built with clinker blocks of different tones, according to the temperature at which they were baked, in a range of colours that cause confusion with the clay soil of the area. It forms terraces which adapt themselves to the topography. It has a continuity in the stairways, in the retaining walls and in the slopes, all paved with the same material.

One of the segments of the «L» corresponds to a half-buried floor where the garage is found and whose roof serves as a large terrace by which the main access to the residence is achieved. The other segment is a building of great simplicity: a long, brick rectangle with a double-pitched roof, with

On the following page, the entrance aspect. The entrance is achieved between the two buildings in a sequential manner. The white-painted, plaster, semi-circular tower stands out from the brick buildings like a swollen candle.

A rear view, in which the white volume of the kitchen with the window onto the coloured garden are outstanding.

Below, an aspect of the clinker block construction, whose image transmits the simplicity of a mountain hermitage or rural construction.

narrow openings and austere finishes. It is a small construction, which, because of its simplicity reminds one more of a mountain hermitage or a barn than a dwelling.

One would say that the architect has thought it necessary to establish a background, in harmony with the landscape, in which to be able to construct another building later.

Occupying the centre of the space in the «L», a semi-circular tower emerges, white and luminous. From the entrance it looks like a great, curved wall, with hardly any openings, which stands out in the middle of the wood like a large screen or a swollen candle. However, the opposite side, completely square, presents a glazed façade, which is open and orientated towards the wood.

The two buildings are joined by the stairway, which thus, converts itself into the centre-piece of the project. Completely glazed, it is constructed from a light, steel framework with wooden steps and is a totally transparent element.

So, even if it forms the link which unites the two buildings, the central element by which all the rooms in the house are related, it is no less true that its very transparent character makes the dual conception of the house more evident. The division of the dwelling, the need to go from one building to the other, becomes evident each time one wishes to go from the living room to the dining room, or from one of the individual bedrooms to the bathroom. Apart from this, since it is a two section stairway, it unites floors at intermediate levels and forces anyone who wishes to go from one building to the other to go up or down half a floor.

This is the spirit of the house. The interior is distributed as a series of areas which do not become distinct rooms. The passageways are split up into short sections which unite intermediate areas. The living room is distinct with respect to the dining room and it does not have precise connection with the entrance hall. Not even the dining room and the kitchen are directly related. The majority of the areas in the house are found in relatively small rooms, spaced out one from the

Detail of the main entrance porch of the dwelling.

Exterior aspect of the living room. The semi-circular building has a different character from one side to the other. The wooden gallery corresponding to the upper-floor bedrooms, supported by a double, central, metal pilar, appears like a stand-alone element which has been incorporated into the composition.

other and separated by distances which incorporate additional events. In fact, in spite of its apparent simplicity, the distribution of the house embodies a large internal complexity, destined to achieve a greater intimateness in the majority of the spaces. The rhythm of the narrowing and the widening, the bends and the spaces which spread out, introduce the magic of places not perfectly defined nor predictable.

The garage is in the basement, also the boiler room, (boilers, washing machine ...), a sauna, workshops and storerooms ... .

The comunal rooms and spaces are on the ground floor. The living room, in the white tower, has been designed as an area completely open to the wood. The paving continues on the other side of the great window, the semi-circular wall, which only closes the room in one direction, leaving the other free.

The dining room is narrow, long and high and it is the only double-space room in the house. The wooden trusses of the ridged roof have been left on view, which introduces the simplicity and sobriety of rural construction into the dining room. On the far side, a stairway allows access to the small loft which has been fitted out as a library. As in the living room, a chimney has become the centre-piece which dominates the room.

The bedrooms are on the first floor, separate in the two buildings. The master bedroom can be found in the brick wing, while three contiguous, individual bedrooms have been constructed in the semi-circular tower, joined by a comunal area which combines the functions of a mere corridor and a small study.

The finishes in the semi-circular building combine the white, plaster surfaces of the curved wall with the glazing of the flat façade, where a wooden gallery overhangs the façade from one extreme to the other.

The openings in the brick building are like small incrustations created in a compact and

hermetic block. The windows are long and narrow. The metal carpentry is lacquered in a dark grey colour, at one extreme of the tone range of the bricks. Both the main access and the entrance to the kitchen from the garden, make use of white plaster walls to reproduce the aesthetics of the semi-circular building and to anticipate the interior finishes. In an identical way, the exterior paving continues in the living rooms, the hall and the dining room.

Cristoph H. Mäckler has been able to introduce, in a not very large house, a diversity of distinct situations, so that each space can be associated with different moments and events. This desire could only be born from a deep appreciation of intimacy and privacy. The very same feelings that would lead a person to choose an out-of-the-way place on a hill, surrounded by trees. •

A view of the stairway which unites the brick building and the semi-circular, white, plaster volume. Since it has two sections, it connects the intermediate floors.

A view of the fireplace in the main building, showing the sloping roofs and exposed wooden beams.

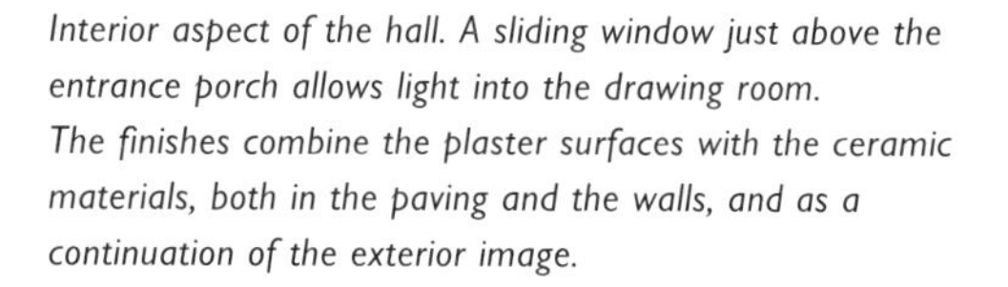

Interior aspect of the hall. A sliding window just above the entrance porch allows light into the drawing room. The finishes combine the plaster surfaces with the ceramic materials, both in the paving and the walls, and as a continuation of the exterior image.

Detail of the corridor which joins the individual bedrooms. The intermediate spaces are exploited by incorporating additional functions.

A view of the area around the hearth in the semi-circular structure: a bright interior, sparingly furnished.

A double-height space containing the piano on the lower level and the library in the loft are connected by a delicate, metal staircase with wooden steps.

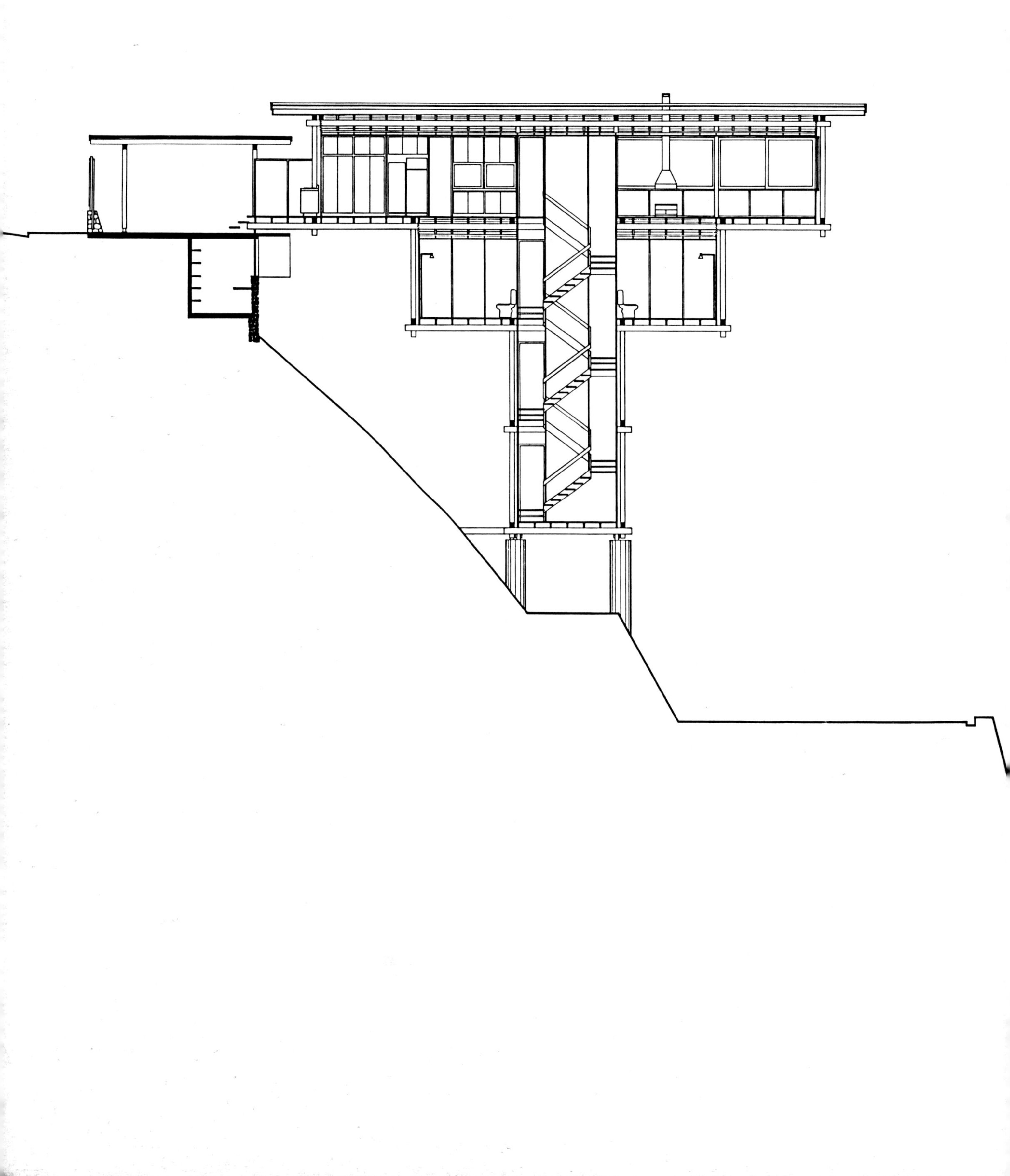

Hélio Olga house

Marcos Acayaba

Sometimes, within the natural context of architecture, an element appears with so much force that, in the end, it manages to attract the very attention which it is trying to diminish. This project exemplifies one of the possible relationships which a house can establish with the terrain when the latter presents a slope that exceeds 45 degrees. It was not in vain that it was conceived as a prototype for very uneven localities, using prefabricated structural elements.

Vehicle access is via the upper level. Marcos Acayaba could not resist the temptation to overfly the cliff.

The project consists of two parts: a tower in form of a " T " and a private terrace which includes the swimming pool and the garage. The terrace, which forms the access plane, rests on the horizontal limit of the plot. The four-storey tower is set on concrete props set into the slope, so that one extreme of the upper floor rests on the terrace. The disposition of the tower, perpendicular to the topographic lines, and its leading to the terrace, can cause the project to be thought of as the beginning of a bridge: the transparency of the upper floor and its condition of a horizontal plane in mid-air, convert going through the dwelling's main room into a stroll along a platform suspended in the air.

There are six props, with a depth of eighteen metres, which protrude from the surface to

delimit the two squares of 3.30 metres that make up the supporting base for the tower. This perimeter is repeated for the two lower floors, the northern half (which is the optimum orientation in the southern hemisphere) corresponds to the rooms, and in the southern half are the services and the staircase. The middle floor has three times the surface and assigns the same functional division to its modules. And finally, the main or upper floor has two more modules on each side, near the terrace.

It consists of an overhanging structure of pillars and wooden beams forming a volumetric reticle whose planes are braced with steel cables in both diagonals. Its symmetry makes it stable by compensation. By minimising the supporting surface, the foundation costs were reduced and the original profile was maintained intact.

Just like a piece of "Mecano", the tower rises, expressing and denouncing the impressive slope of the terrain, with which it maintains only a few points of contact. That of the terrace offers a greater security margin of stability against the force of the south winds. In the base, behind an exit door in the lower floor, there is a simple bridge set into the ground.

The exterior is enlightening. The house's façades show and explain its interior workings, its construction and the concepts of its structure. While the metallic guys cross in front and the

By night, the city gains life in the background and the dwelling reveals its intimacy.

The uniqueness of the slope. In a context characterised by the terrain, the colours are outstanding, and also the materials, but above all, the expressive force of a form resolved by techno-constructive resources normally reserved for other purposes.

Lower view from the north. The structure of a bridge applied to a conventional programme.

An aerial view of the countryside next to the façade of the house. Girders and wooden beams are superimposed to form frameworks, leaving on view the space which remains between them. Most of the façade's modules present a parapet formed of three white panels and wood carpentry which divides the upper part in two. The drainpipes are suspended from the plane of the roof.

While the house moves towards empty space, the terrace remains behind, on one side, attached to the ground. The swimming pool is situated at the limit of the descent.

Lower frontal view. The contrasted combination of materials.

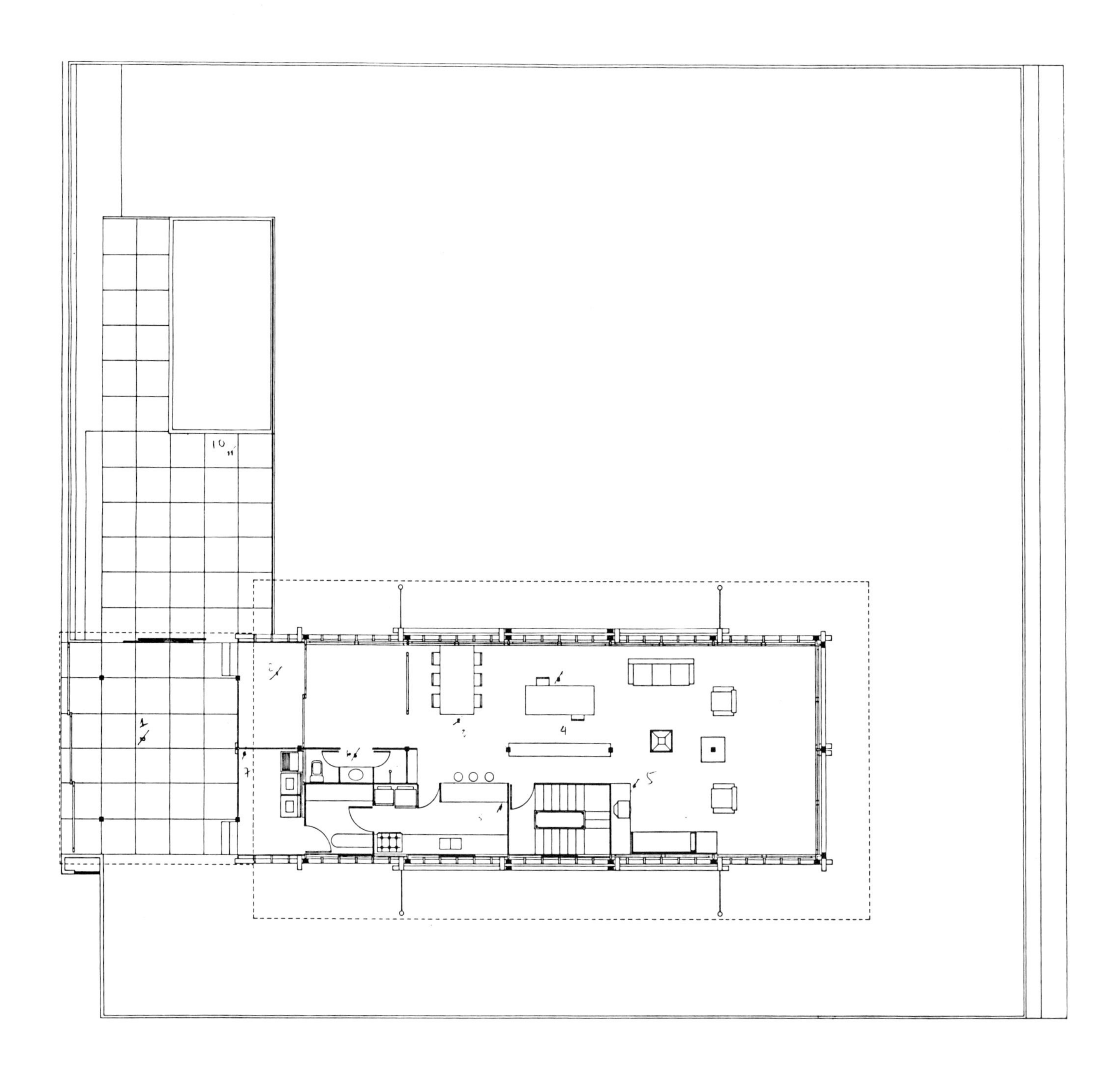

The perpendicularity of main floor (level 0.00). With the services grouped on one side, the succession of furniture through free space, based on modules, defines the different areas (hall, dining room, library, and living room).

The garage's canopy rests on the metal base of four wooden pillars. The translucence insinuates the outside on both sides, and in the background, the interior of the house.

Construction details of the anchorage of the pillars on the concrete props; of the superposition of the wooden beams on the girders using metal flats; and the fixing of the struts.

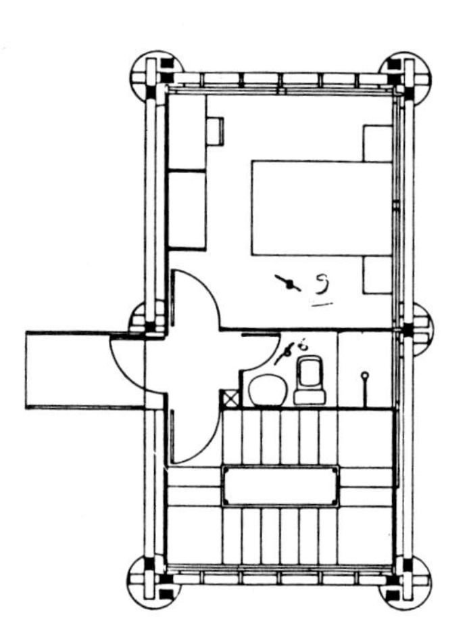

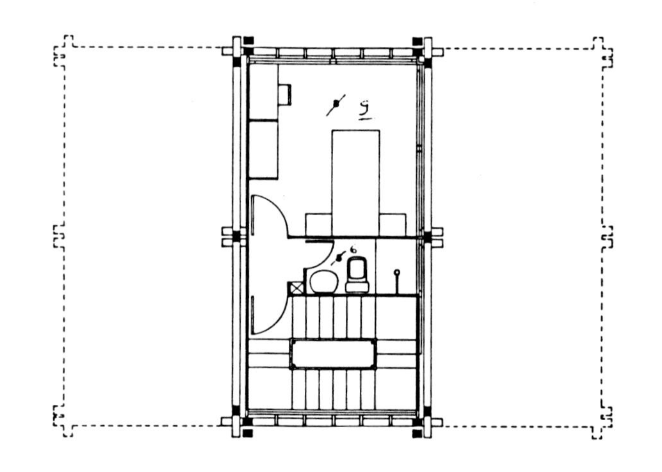

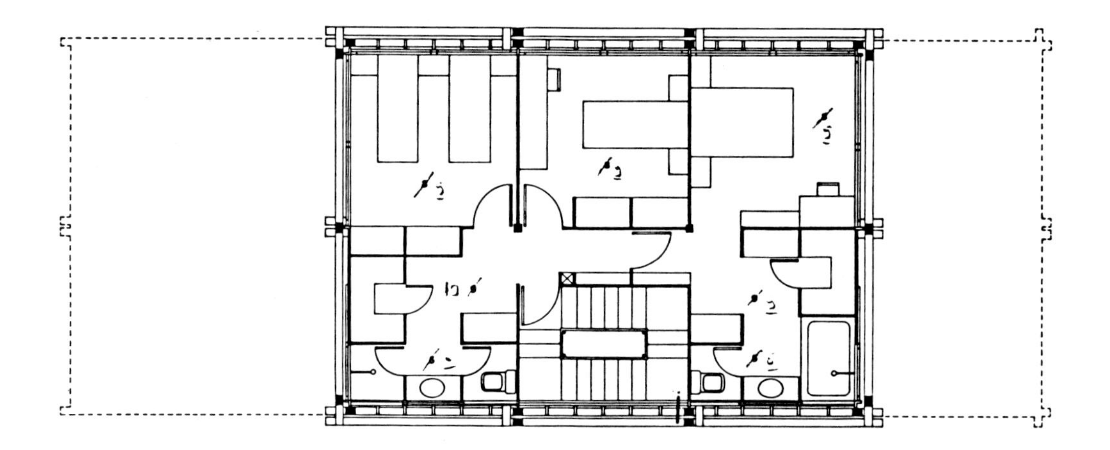

The middle (level -3.30) and lower floors (levels -6.60 and -9.90) with the same functional division applied to their modules.

Wood is predominant in the living room: furniture, floor, roof, carpentry and structure. The pillars of the central porch form a base which distributes the forces. The chimney is suspended from the roof in the same way as the drainpipes.

wooden joists appear outside, the blinds combine with the partitions in geometrical modules, thus identifying each one of the rooms.

The plane of the roof overhangs the whole, and incorporates details which convert the work of engineering into poetry. Four metal tubes hang in the air in the lateral extremes: rainwater is scattered by the wind, re-affirming the voluntary impartiality of the terrain.

The parapets serve as support for the furniture, favouring the visual continuity with nature, and is only interrupted by the service area. The wooden boards mark the length of the space.